G000065624

The Complete Rock Guitar Player.

by Steve Tarshis.

Book One.

Amsco Publications
New York/London/Sydney/Cologne

Photographs:

Robert Matthew/Retna Ltd.	6
Michael Putland/Retna Ltd.	8, 20
Beth Gwinn/Retna Ltd.	10
Andrea Laubach/Retna Ltd.	12
David Redfern/Retna Ltd.	14, 18, 22
Janette Beckman/Retna Ltd.	16
Walter McBride/Retna Ltd.	25

Edited by Peter Pickow
Interior layout and design by Leonard Vogler
Illustrative photography by M. Butler and A. Kopp

International Standard Book Number: 0.8256.1072.9

Exclusive Distributors:
Music Sales Corporation
24 East 22nd Street, New York, NY 10010 USA
Music Sales Limited
8/9 Frith Street, London W1V 5TZ England
Music Sales Pty. Limited
120 Rothschild Street, Rosebery, Sydney, NSW 2018, Australia

Printed in the United States of America by
Vicks Lithograph and Printing Corporation

Contents

The Songs

About This Book

This is the first book of an exciting new series for the aspiring rock guitarist. You will learn from a unique perspective. Right from the beginning you will be playing some of the greatest rock songs ever written; songs made famous by the all-time greats; from Chuck Berry to the Police.

You will learn the basic material that all guitarists need to know, but you will also learn those techniques which are unique to rock music.

You can use this book on your own, in a classroom, or with a private teacher. The notation, especially at the beginning, is simple and easy to follow. The words to the songs are also included.

So here it is. With a little practice, I think you can have some fun and get a pretty good start on rock 'n' roll guitar.

Holding the Guitar

Many rock 'n' roll guitarists have developed their own styles of holding their instruments, but basically, the guitar is held as shown below.

Sitting position:

Standing position:

The right hand is used for strumming. Hold the pick between the thumb and first finger, as shown below.

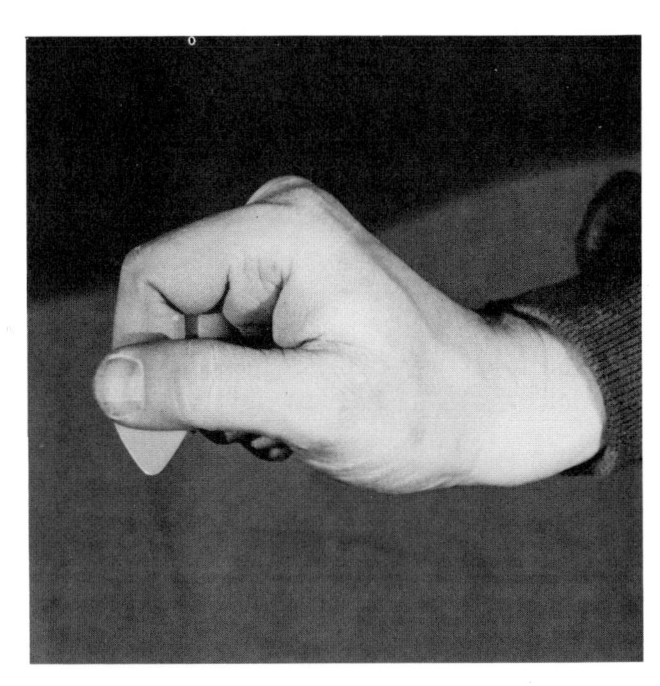

The left hand is used to press the strings of the guitar down onto the fretboard to play notes and chords.

The crook of the right arm rests on the corner of the guitar so that the forearm can strum freely. The right hand falls over the strings at the sound hold (acoustic guitar) or at the pickups (electric guitar).

The left hand should hang freely also. Try not to rest your left elbow on your knee when sitting.

Tuning the Guitar

Before each playing session, you must tune your guitar. Many guitarists use electronic tuners. These are small devices (they fit in your case) which are not too expensive. They are especially useful for electric guitars.

There is also a method known as relative tuning. With this method you tune the guitar to itself. Estimate the correct pitch of the sixth, or E, string (the lowest sounding string). Play the fifth fret of the sixth string and listen to the sound. Tune the open fifth string up or down until it matches that sound. Now play the fifth fret of the fifth string, and tune the open fourth string to that sound. Next play the fifth fret of the fourth string, and tune the open third string to that sound. Now play the third string at the fourth fret, and tune the open second string to that sound. Finally, play the fifth fret of the second string, and tune the open first string to that sound.

Parts of the Guitar

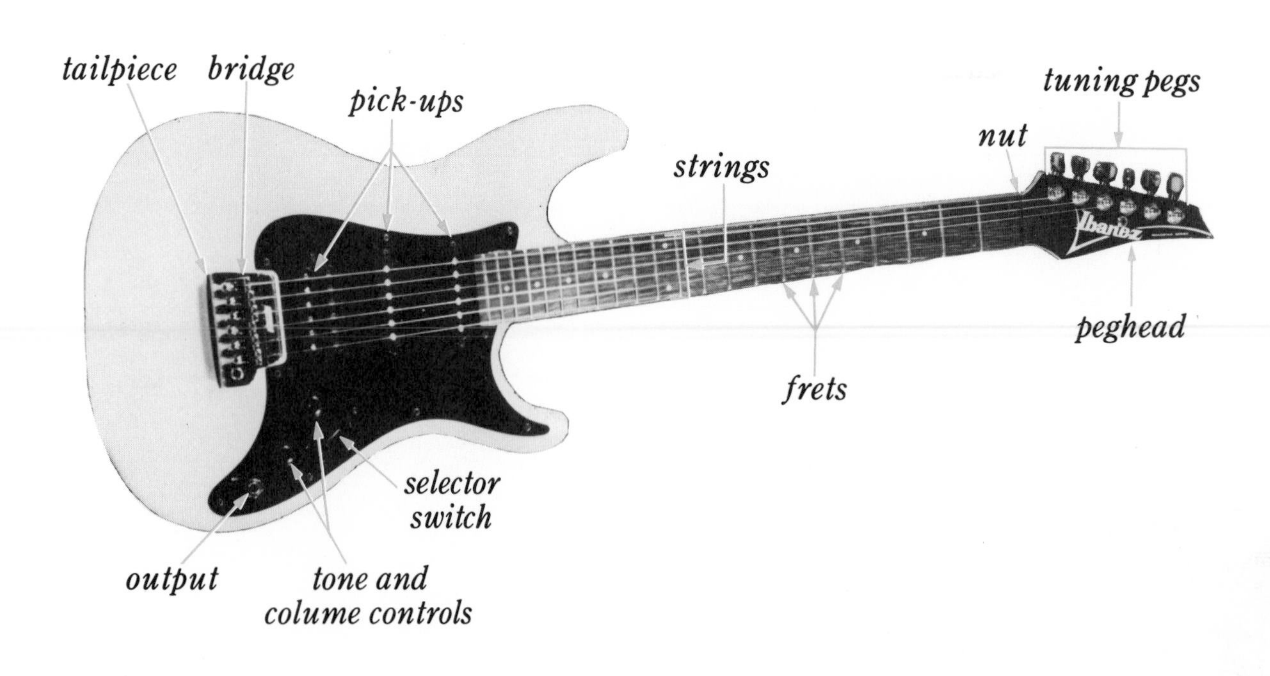
tailpiece
bridge
pick-ups
strings
nut
tuning pegs
peghead
frets
selector switch
output
tone and colume controls

The Basic Strum

The heart of rock 'n' roll has always been the beat, and the heart of rock 'n' roll guitar is the rhythm. Without a good rhythm, even a good song can sound bad. The opposite is also true: With a good rocking rhythm, almost anything can sound good.

For a rock guitar player, the rhythm lies in the right hand, the hand that holds the pick. For this reason, the first thing we're going to work on is a right-hand strum that will always work—a "machine" that we can turn on and will always run, regardless of what the left hand is doing. For now, the left hand won't be doing anything: for this basic right-hand exercise you will be strumming the open strings.

The basic strum is a constant up-and-down motion. The pick is held between the thumb and first finger of the right hand and brushed against the strings. Try not to touch the wood of the guitar with the pick. The strings are as close as the pick gets to the guitar.

Most rock rhythms can be broken down into groups of four beats. As indicated in the notation below, play a downstroke for each number and an upstroke for the **and** after each number. Practice this strum slowly and evenly—what is important is not the speed, but the steadiness of the strum.

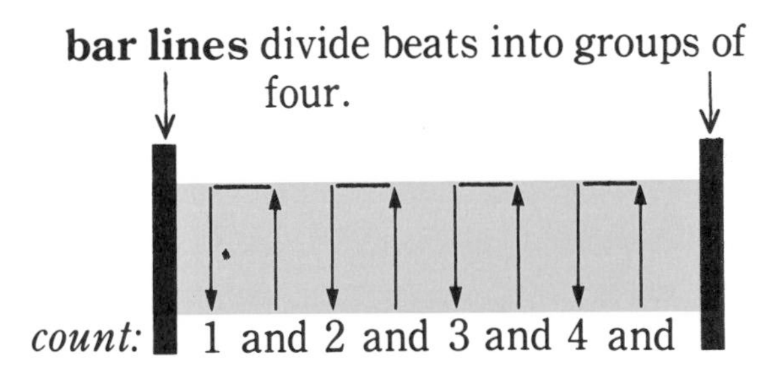
bar lines divide beats into groups of four.
count:
1 and 2 and 3 and 4 and

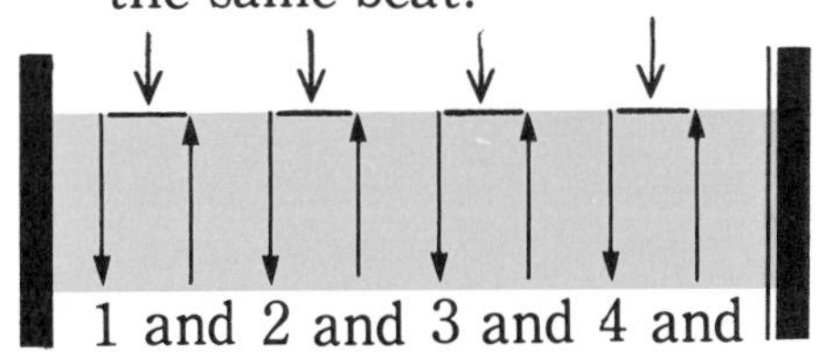
beams join strums that occur within the same beat.
1 and 2 and 3 and 4 and

Chords

In order to start making music with our basic strum, we have to learn a few chords. You can think of chords as shapes that are formed with the fingers of the left hand on the neck of the guitar. I'm going to show you how to play these shapes by using a **chord diagram.** The neck of the guitar will be shown like this:

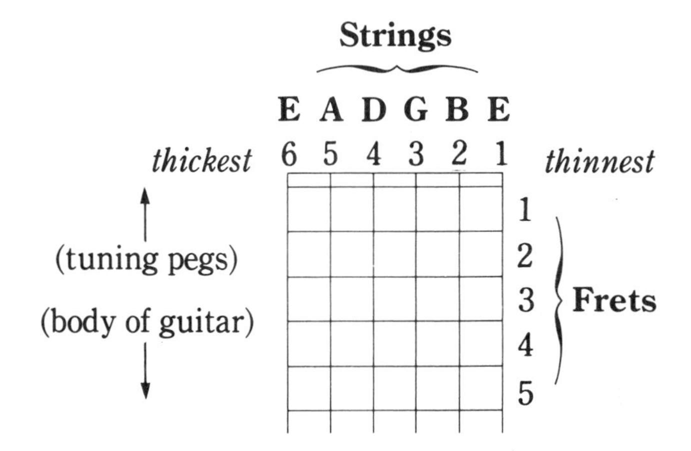
Strings
E A D G B E
thickest
6 5 4 3 2 1
thinnest
(tuning pegs)
(body of guitar)
1
2
3
4
5
Frets

Our first chord will be **E Minor (Em).** It is played by placing the fingers of the left hand on the neck of the guitar as shown in the diagram below. The fingers of the left hand are numbered as follows:

1 = index finger
2 = middle finger
3 = ring finger
4 = pinky

Em

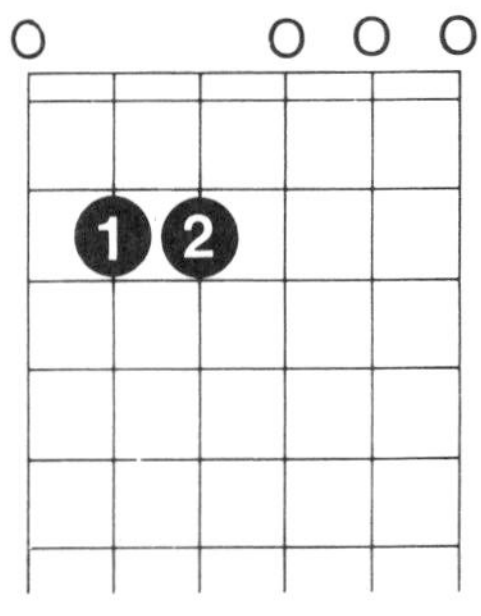
1
2

A circle indicates that the string is played open.

Miss You

When fingering a note on the guitar, position each finger as close to the metal fret bar as possible without actually touching it. (Touching the metal fret bar will give you a buzzing sound.) The diagram below shows the correct finger placement for the **Em** chord.

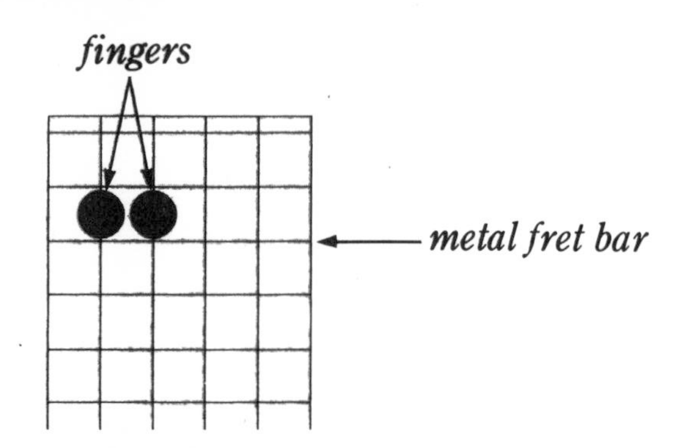
fingers
metal fret bar

Press down firmly with the first and second fingers of the left hand, and start your right-hand machine. As indicated in the notation below, strum the **Em** chord sixteen times (eight down-up motions), then strum the open strings sixteen times. Keep repeating this until you can do it smoothly. Remember, the idea is to keep the right-hand machine going, without stopping, while the left-hand fingers go on and off the neck.

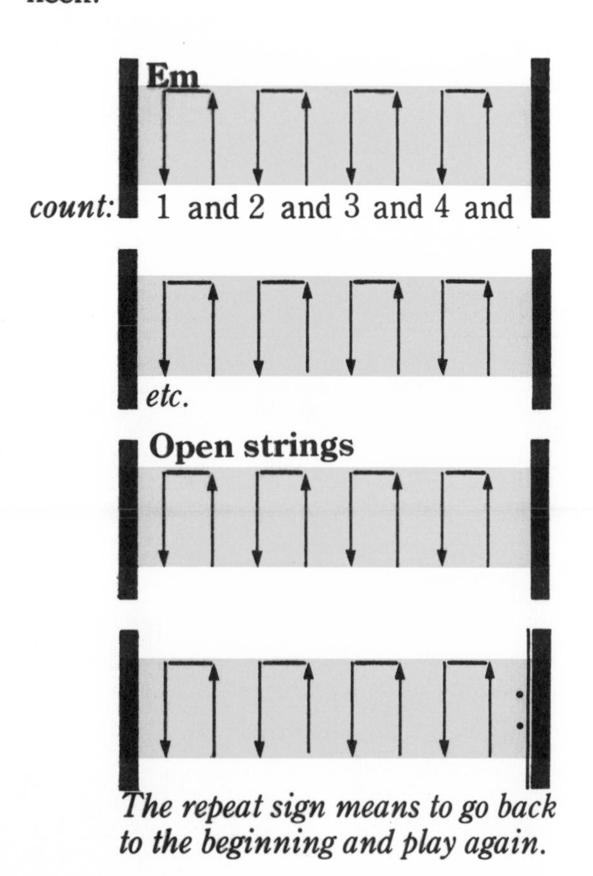
Em
count: 1 and 2 and 3 and 4 and
etc.
Open strings

The repeat sign means to go back to the beginning and play again.

With one more chord we can start playing some songs. Look at the diagram below and finger an **A Minor Seventh** chord **(Am7).**

Am7

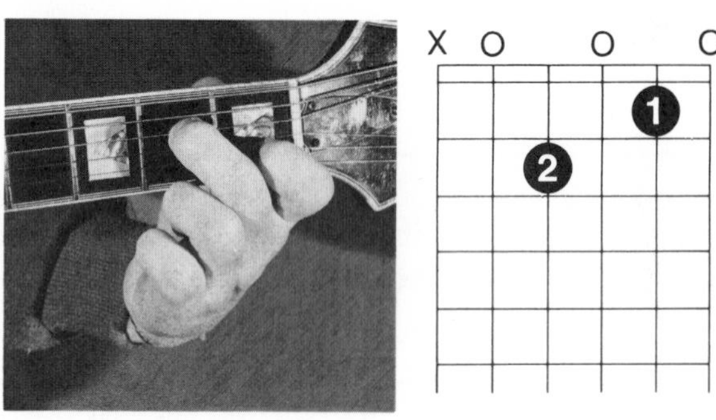
X O O O
1
2

An x indicates that the string is not played.

Practice playing **Am7** using the basic strum. Then practice alternating between **Am7** and the open strings (sixteen times each). Remember, keep that right-hand machine going!

Now we're ready to play our first song, the Rolling Stones' "Miss You." To play this song we will move back and forth between **Em** and **Am7**. When switching from **Em** to **Am7**, hold the second finger down and move only the first finger. Each chord will receive sixteen strums (two groups of four beats). Each group of four beats is known as a **measure** of music.

Miss You
Words and Music by Mick Jagger and Keith Richards

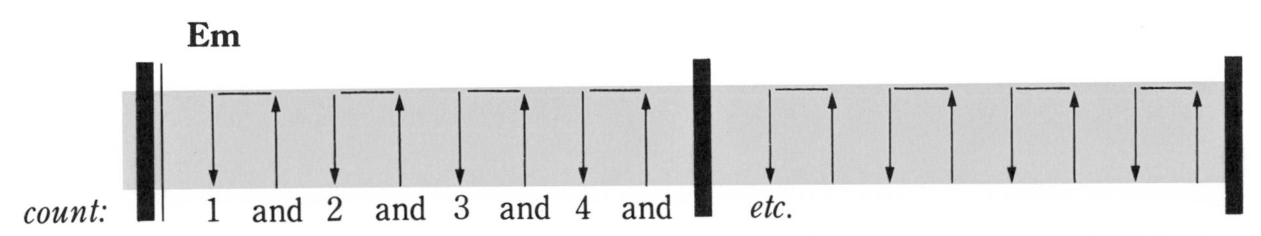
Em
count: 1 and 2 and 3 and 4 and etc.

1. I've been hold-ing out so long,___ I've been sleep-ing all a-lone.___ Girl, I
(2.) ooh ooh ooh ooh ooh, ooh ooh ooh ooh ooh ooh ooh, ooh ooh

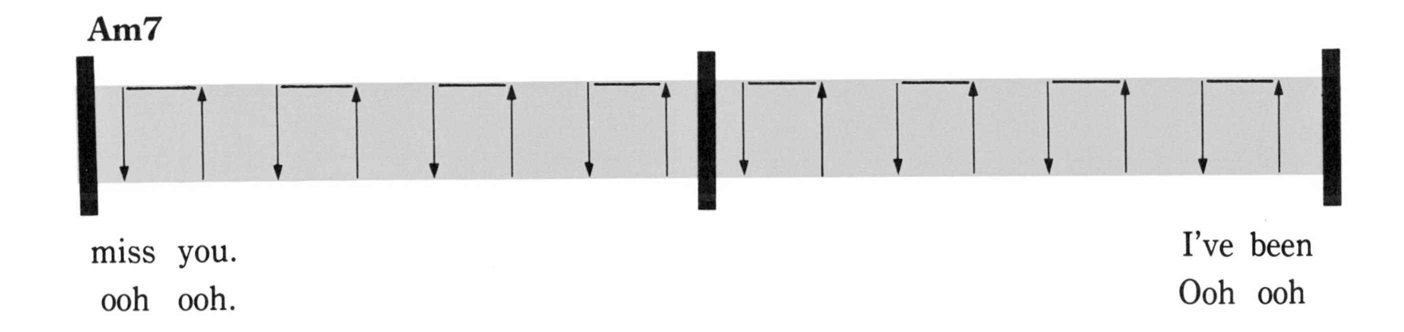
Am7

miss you. I've been
ooh ooh. Ooh ooh

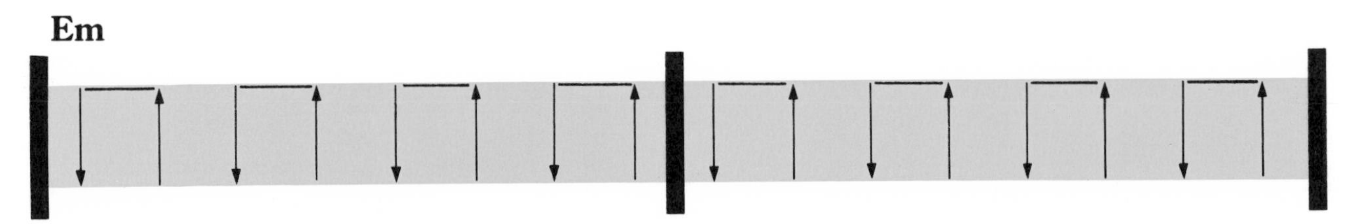
Em

hang-ing on the phone,___ I've been sleep-ing all a - lone. I wan - na
ooh ooh ooh ooh ooh, ooh ooh ooh ooh ooh ooh ooh, ooh ooh ooh

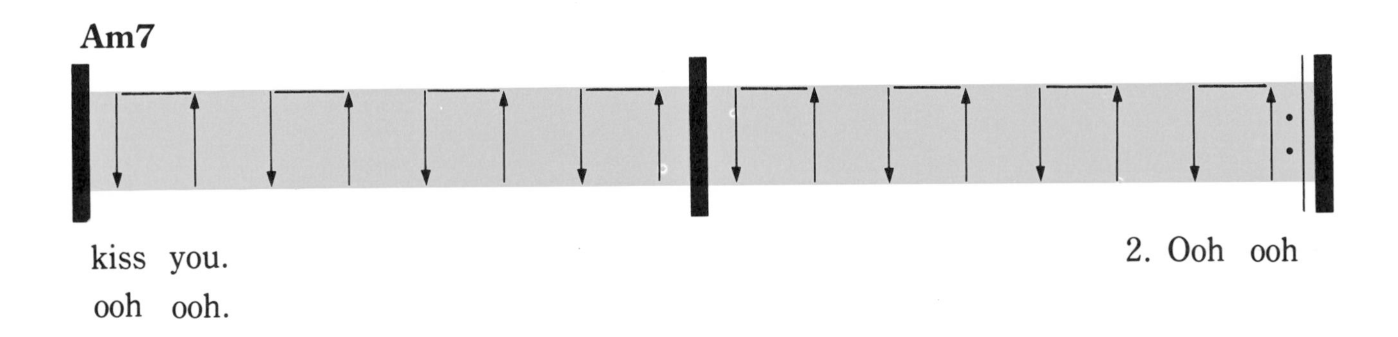
Am7

kiss you. 2. Ooh ooh
ooh ooh.

Shout

Let's learn two more chords, **C Major Seventh (Cmaj7)** and **A,** and play another song.

Cmaj7

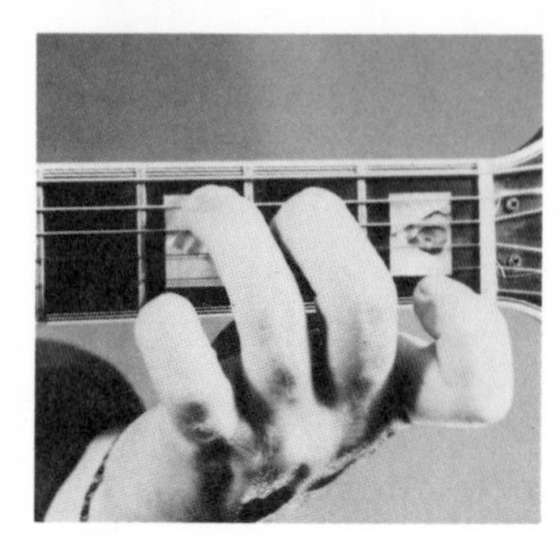

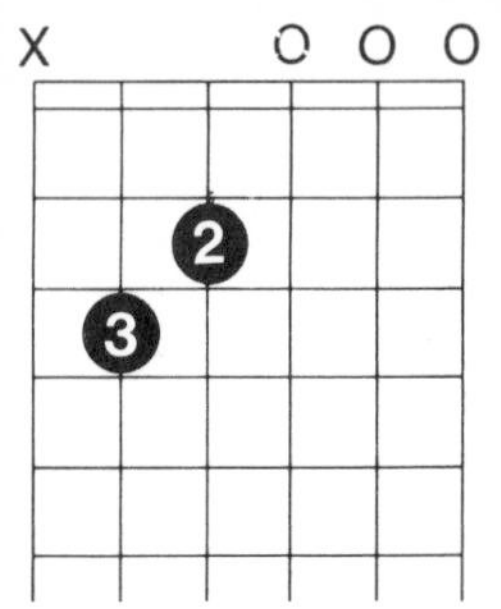
X O O O
2
3

A

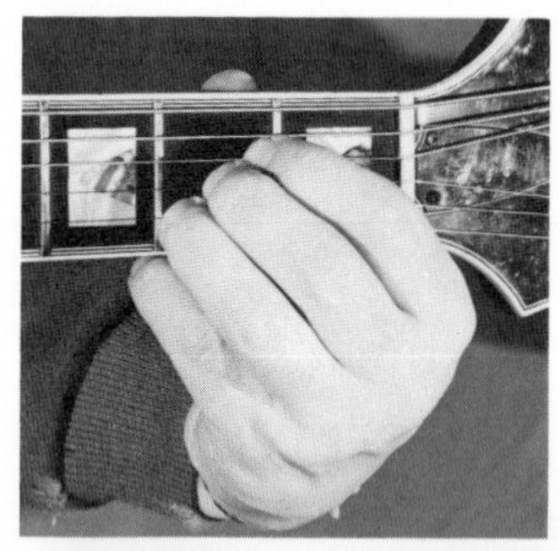

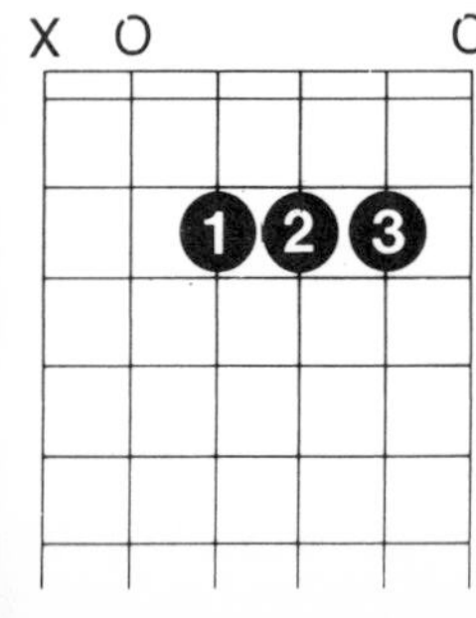
X O O
1 2 3

Practice these chords using the basic strum. Then practice alternating between each chord and the open strings. (Sixteen strums each) until you feel comfortable with them.

Remember, when you change chords, move only those fingers that will be on a new string or fret. For example, when moving from **Em** to **Cmaj7**, your second finger can stay where it is.

Here's another tip: When moving from **A** to **Em**, think of the first and second fingers as a unit and move them simultaneously.

Once you are ready to move the chords while strumming with the right hand, try to adopt the "machine" attitude. In other words, don't get in the habit of stopping your strumming to give yourself time to make the chord changes. Your right hand should keep going no matter what, even if the left hand is stumbling a bit. Remember, the rhythm should be your first concern when playing rock 'n' roll.

Now let's try the Tears for Fears song "Shout." Use the same down-up motion you used in "Miss You."

Shout

Words and Music by Roland Orzabel and Ian Stanley.

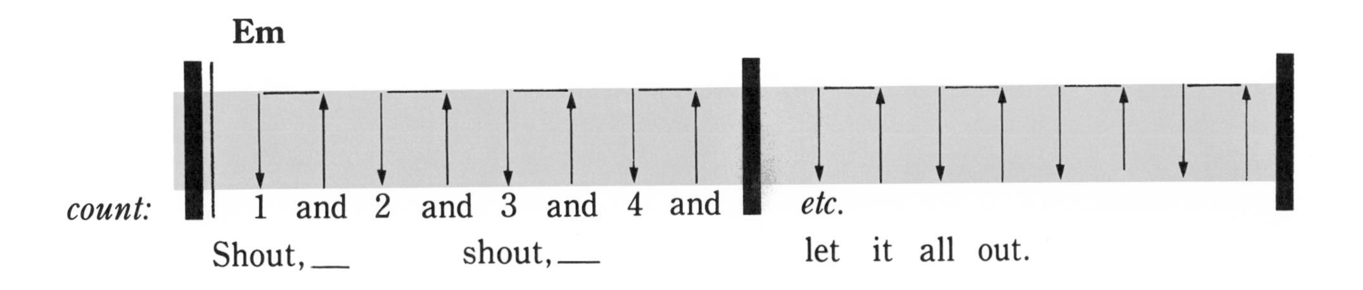
Em
count: 1 and 2 and 3 and 4 and *etc.*
Shout, __ shout, __ let it all out.

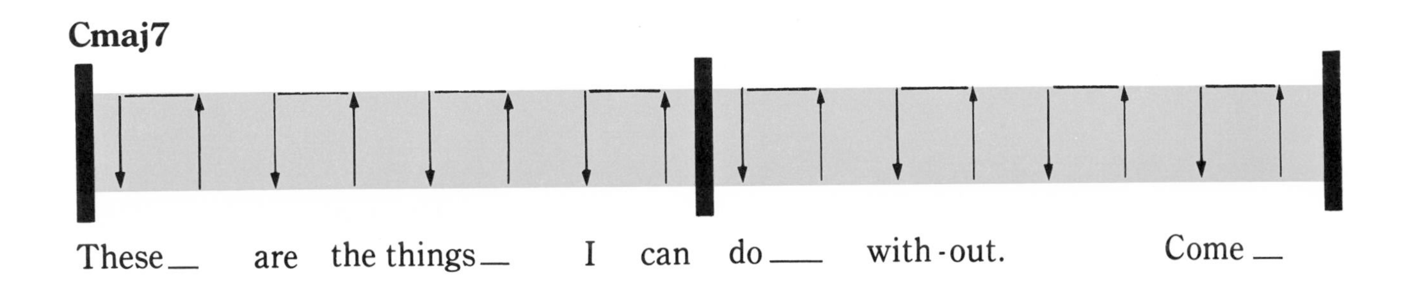
Cmaj7
These __ are the things __ I can do __ with - out. Come __

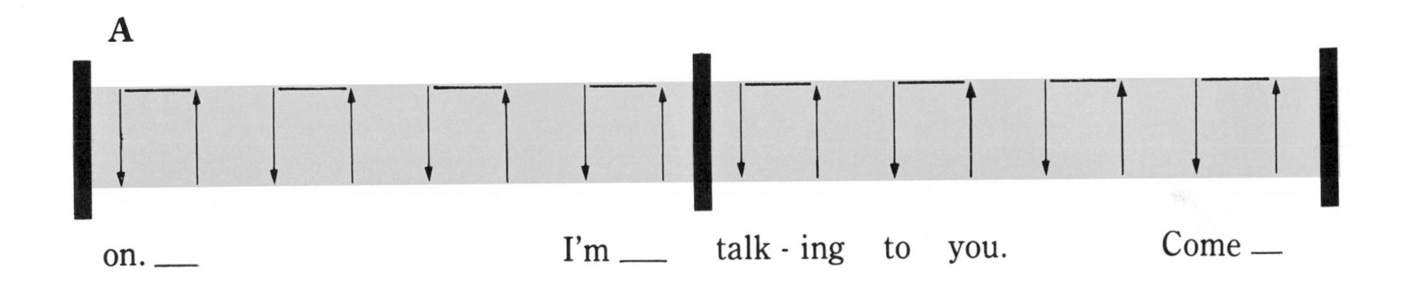
A
on. __ I'm __ talk - ing to you. Come __

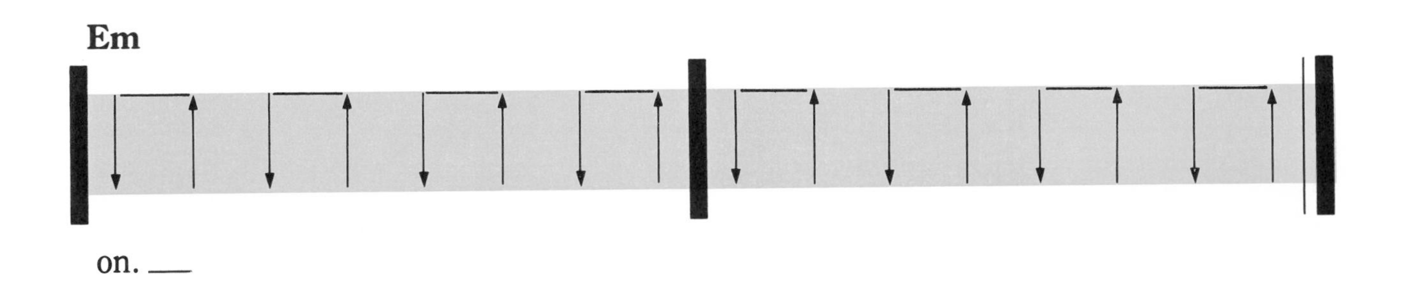
Em
on. __

Down by the River

Look at the diagram below and play a D7 chord.

D7

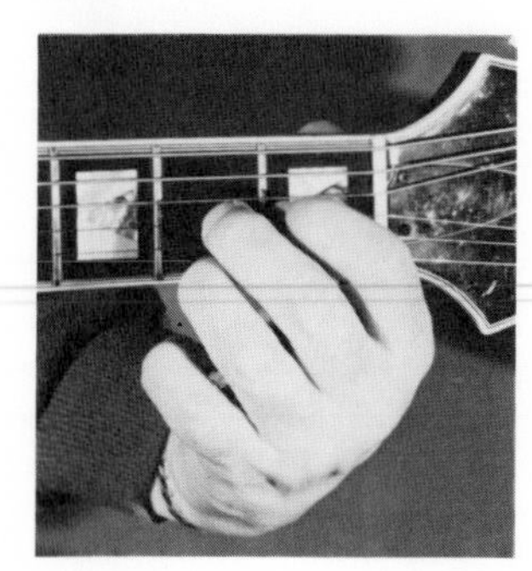

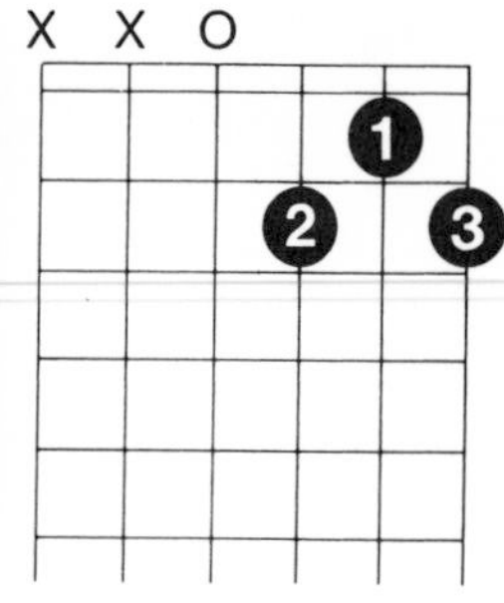

X X O
1
2
3

With the **Am7** chord and the **D7** chord we can play Neil Young's "Down by the River." First I want to show you a new strum. For this song, instead of strumming in a constant down-up, down-up pattern, we will use a down, down, down-up, down-up pattern. The important thing to realize when playing this pattern is that the first two downstrokes take up the first two full beats, or the same amount of time that two down-up strums take in the basic strum (**Strumming Pattern 1**). You can compare the two patterns in the notation below. Notice that beats three and four are the same in each pattern.

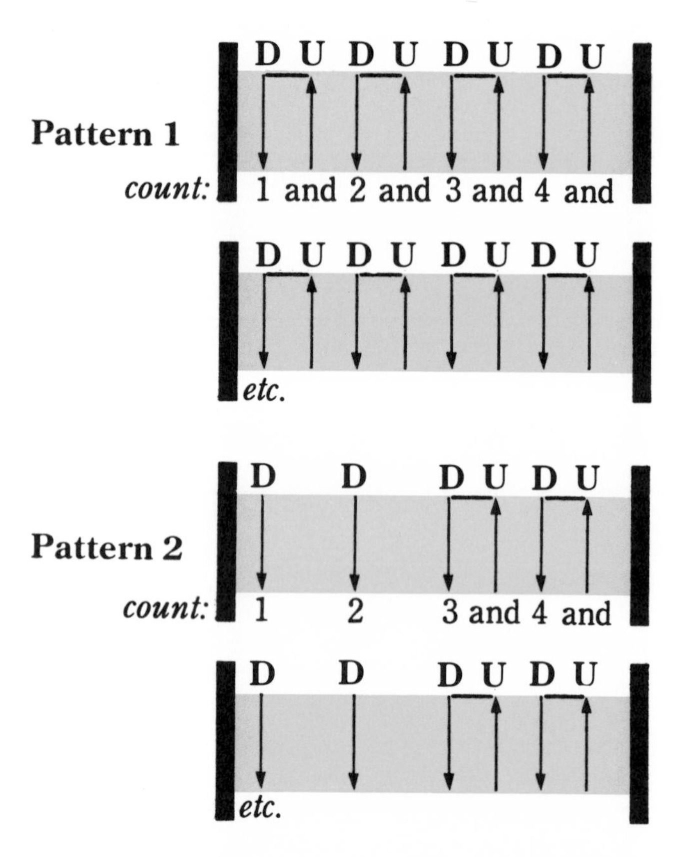

Pattern 1
D U D U D U D U
count: 1 and 2 and 3 and 4 and
D U D U D U D U
etc.
Pattern 2
D D D U D U
count: 1 2 3 and 4 and
D D D U D U
etc.

For "Down by the River," use **Strumming Pattern 2** and play one measure each of **Am7** and **D7.** Remember, when switching back and forth between **Am7** and **D7**, don't move the first finger at all. Move the other fingers in one motion, and keep the strum going no matter what!

Down by the River
Words and Music by Neil Young

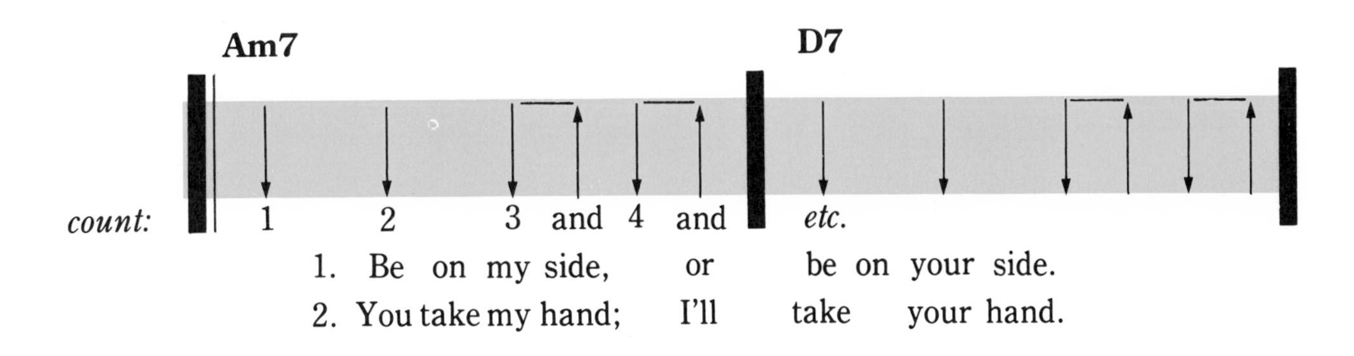
Am7
D7
count: 1 2 3 and 4 and etc.
1. Be on my side, or be on your side.
2. You take my hand; I'll take your hand.

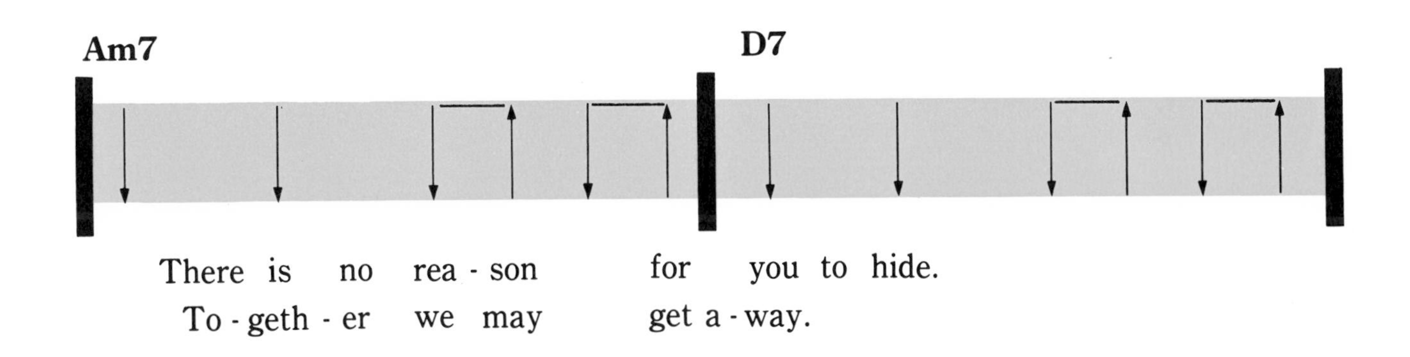
Am7
D7
There is no rea - son for you to hide.
To - geth - er we may get a - way.

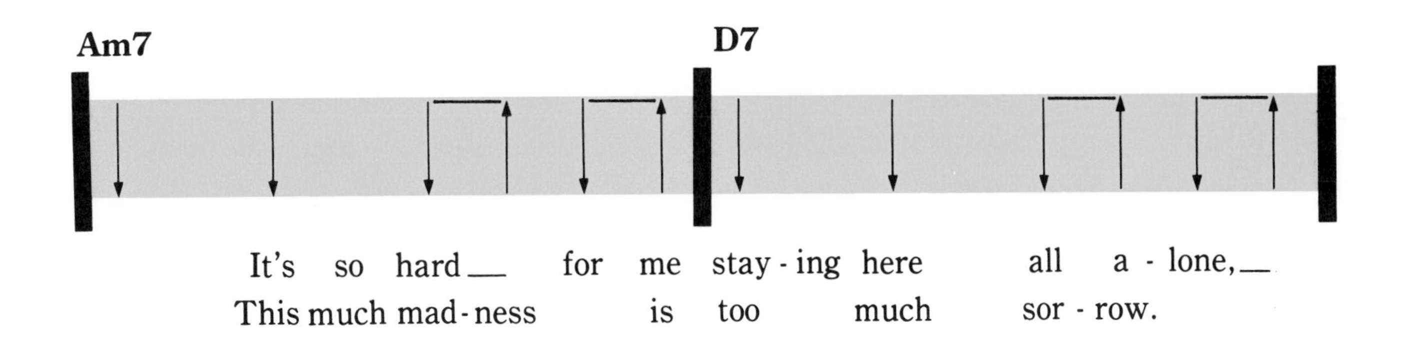
Am7
D7
It's so hard__ for me stay - ing here all a - lone,__
This much mad - ness is too much sor - row.

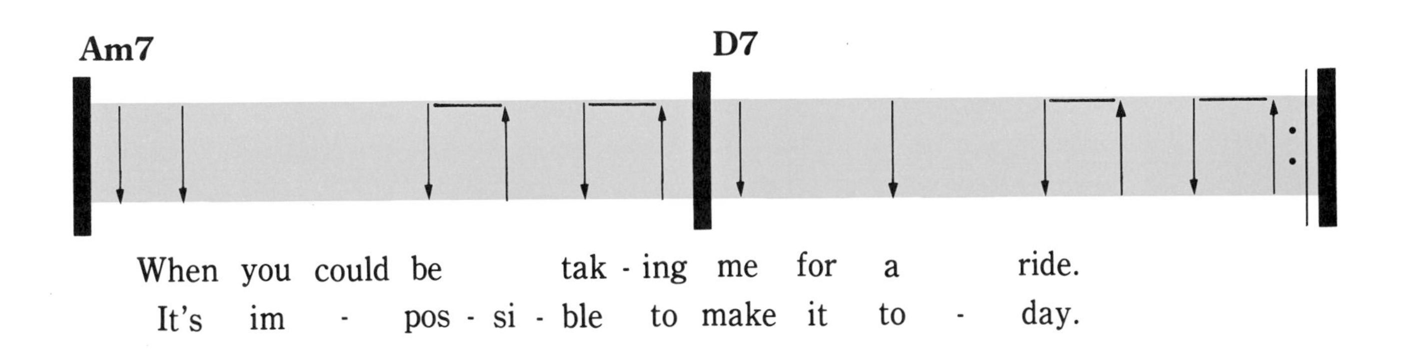
Am7
D7
When you could be tak - ing me for a ride.
It's im - pos - si - ble to make it to - day.

From Me to You

Not let's learn two new chords so we can play a classic Beatles song, "From Me to You."

C

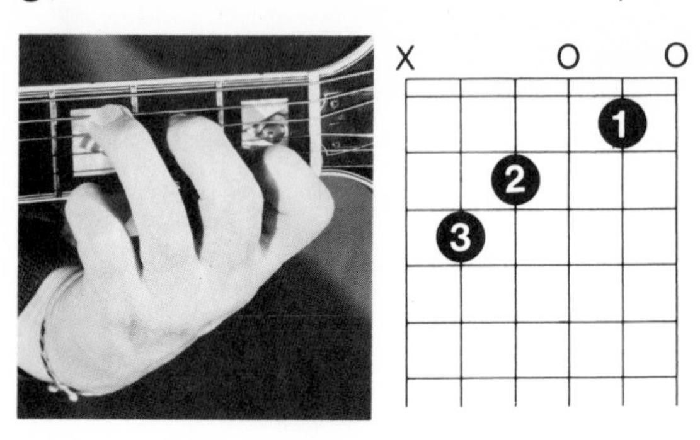
X O O
1
2
3

G

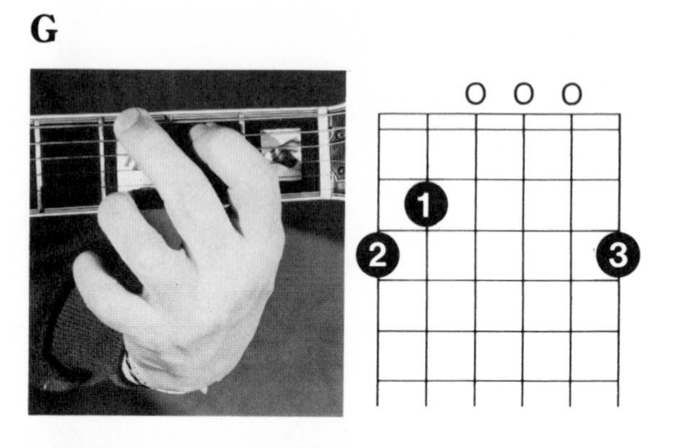
O O O
1
2
3

The fingering for the **C** chord is the same as the fingering for **Am7**, except that your third finger is added at the third fret of the fifth string.

Many songs that use the **C** chord also use the **G** chord. When you practice the **G** chord, make sure your left-hand fingers don't muffle the sound of the open second, third, and fourth strings. This is an important chord in rock music, so make sure it has a good, clean sound.

Use Strumming Pattern 2 to play "From Me to You."

THE
BEATLES

From Me to You

Words and Music by John Lennon and Paul McCartney

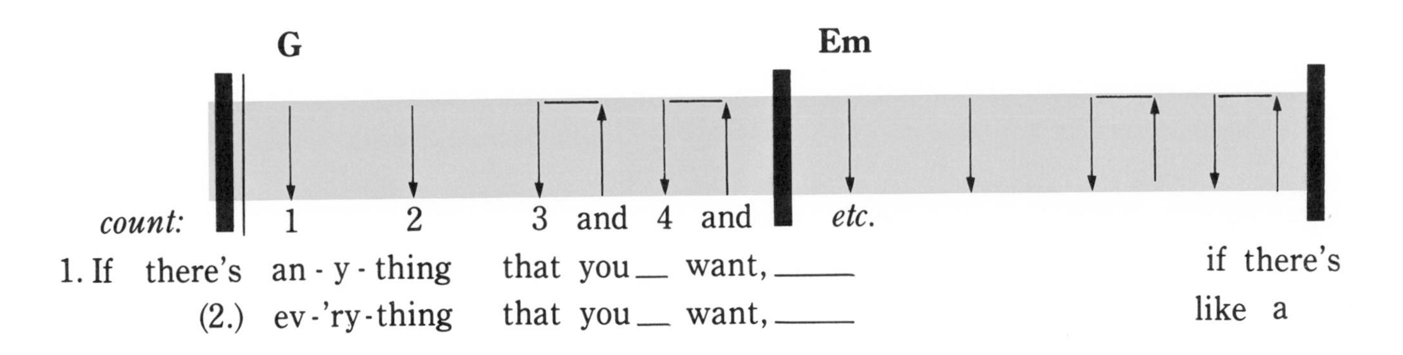
G
Em
count: 1 2 3 and 4 and etc.
1. If there's an - y - thing that you want, if there's
(2.) ev - 'ry - thing that you want, like a

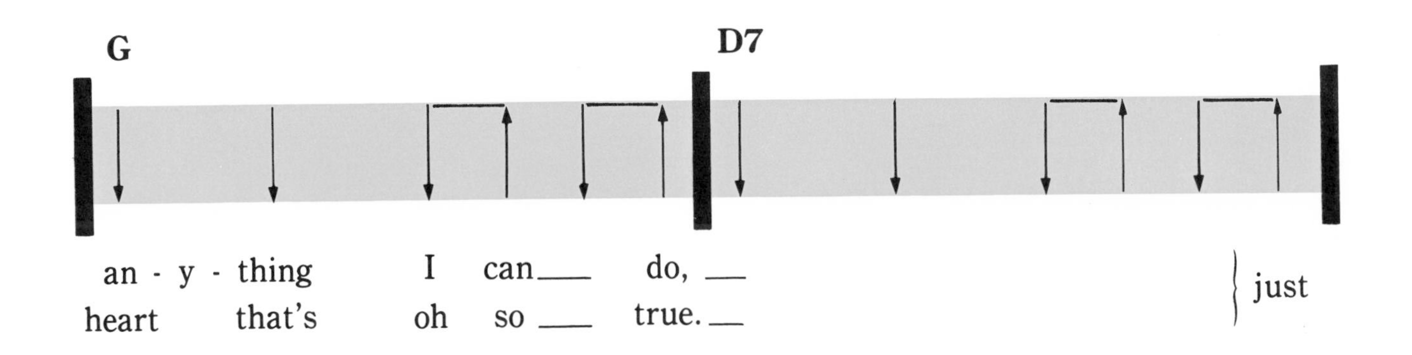
G
D7
an - y - thing I can do, just
heart that's oh so true.

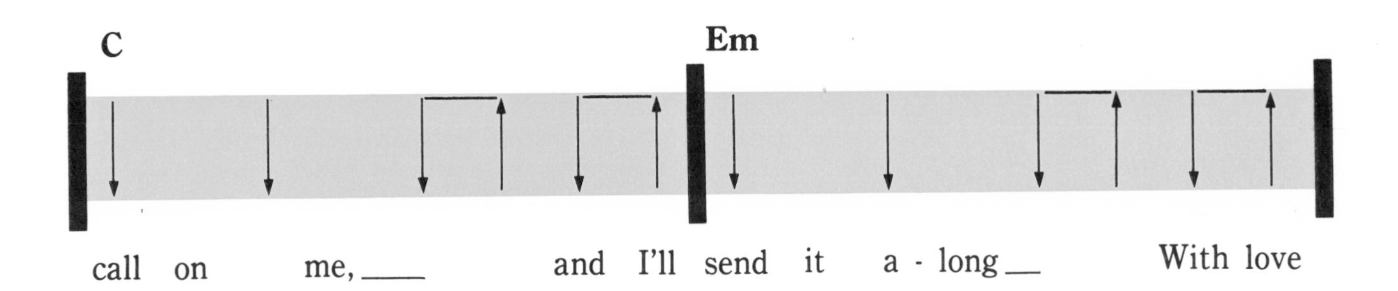
C
Em
call on me, and I'll send it a - long With love

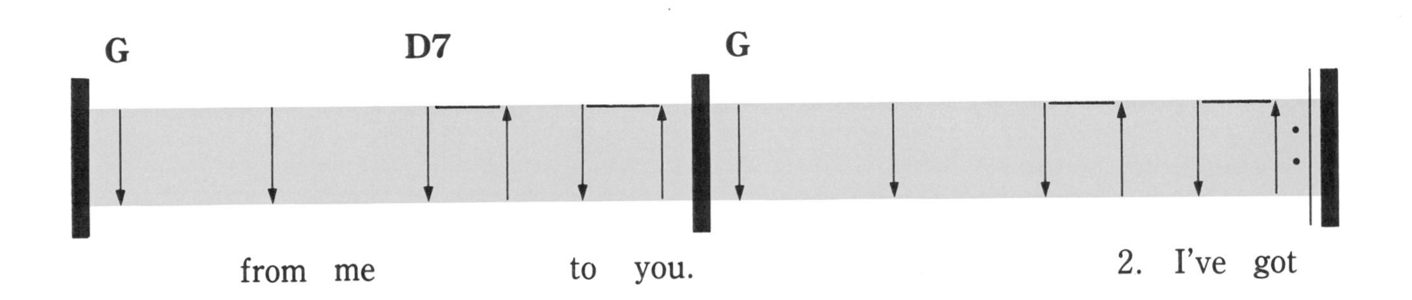
G
D7
G
from me to you. 2. I've got

Roxanne

To play "Roxanne," by the Police, you need to learn two new chords, **D** and **Bm.**

D

X X O

Bm

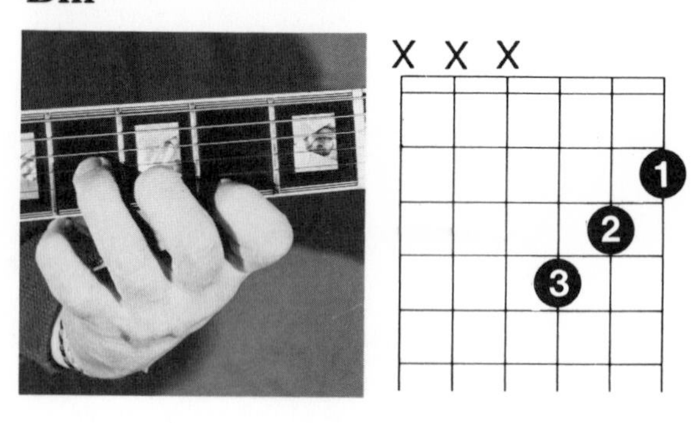
X X X

You can play exactly the same strum that's used on the recording by playing only downstrokes (one on each beat). Sometimes, as indicated in the notation below, you'll strum a chord and let it ring for two full measures. In the chorus section, use the basic strum (down-up on each beat).

Roxanne

Words and Music by The Police

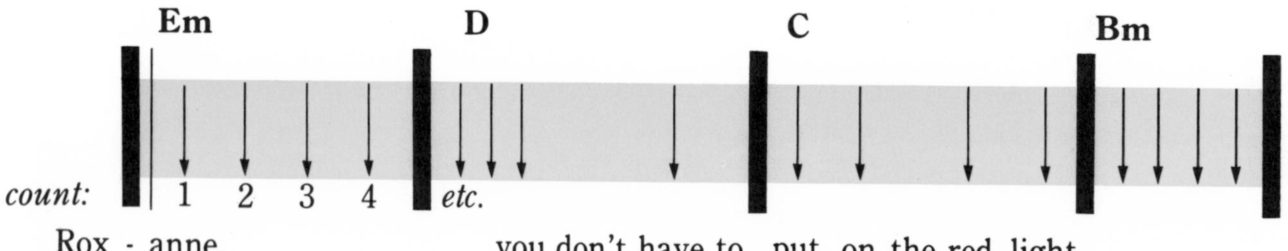
Em
D
C
Bm
count:
1 2 3 4
etc.

Rox - anne, you don't have to put on the red light.

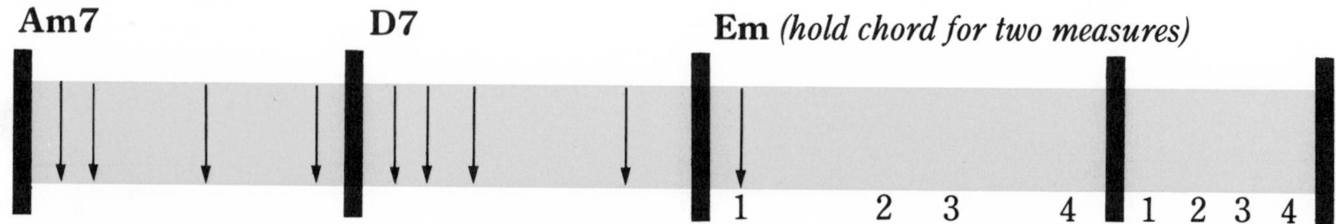
Am7
D7
Em (hold chord for two measures)
1 2 3 4
1 2 3 4

Those days are o - ver. You don't have to sell your body to the night. Rox -

Roxanne *continued*

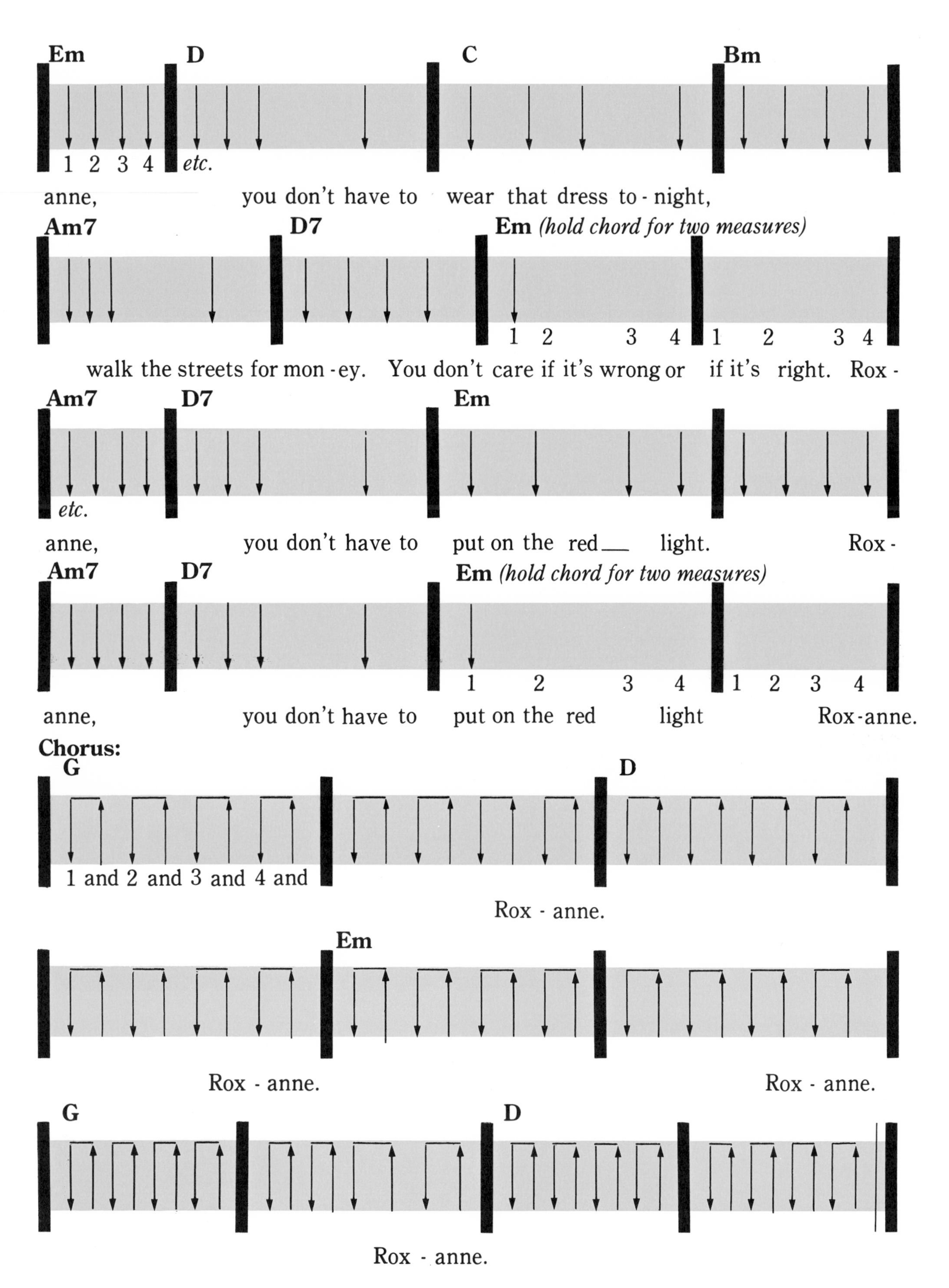

Em
D
C
Bm
1 2 3 4
etc.
anne, you don't have to wear that dress to-night,
Am7
D7
Em (hold chord for two measures)
1 2 3 4
1 2 3 4
walk the streets for mon-ey. You don't care if it's wrong or if it's right. Rox-
Am7
D7
Em
etc.
anne, you don't have to put on the red___ light. Rox-
Am7
D7
Em (hold chord for two measures)
1 2 3 4
1 2 3 4
anne, you don't have to put on the red light Rox-anne.
Chorus:
G
D
1 and 2 and 3 and 4 and
Rox - anne.
Em
Rox - anne.
Rox - anne.
G
D
Rox - anne.

Great Balls of Fire

One of the original wild men of rock is rockabilly master Jerry Lee Lewis. Many of his recordings have become rock 'n' roll classics. I'd like to teach you one of them, the irresistible "Great Balls of Fire."

First we need to learn a new chord, **E7**

E7

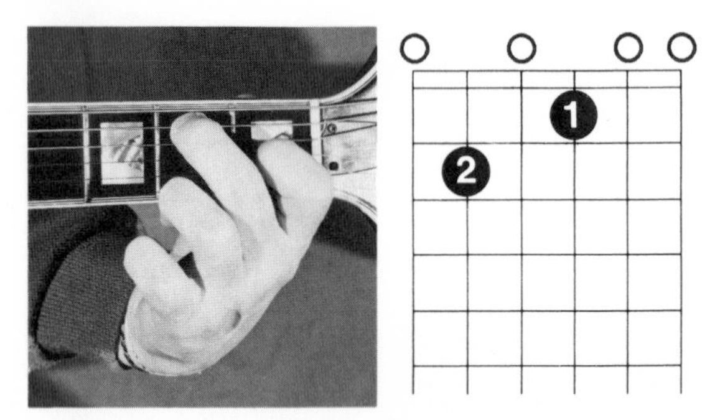

You can play this song with a down-up, down-up, down-up, down-up pattern; but once you get the chords going, I'd like you to try a strumming variation to make the song rock a little bit more. In this variation you will make a percussive sound. Place your right-hand palm against the strings, near the bridge. With your wrist only, brush the strings as if you were playing a regular chord. This should produce a sound that sounds like "chick." Now, finger any chord. Play the down-up, down-up, down-up, down-up rhythm, except on the second and fourth "down," press your palm against the strings and play the "chick" sound. This will give you a rhythm that sounds as if a drummer is playing along on the second and fourth beat.

The exercise below will help you get into it. It takes a little bit of practice, but this technique can really juice up your playing.

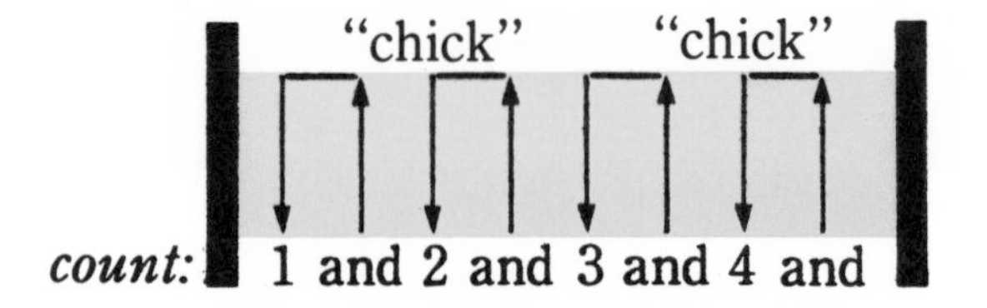
"chick"
"chick"
count:
1 and 2 and 3 and 4 and

Let's try out this new technique on "Great Balls of Fire." As indicated in the notation below, strum the last chord once and let it ring for two measures.

Great Balls of Fire

Words and Music by Otis Blackwell and Jack Hammer

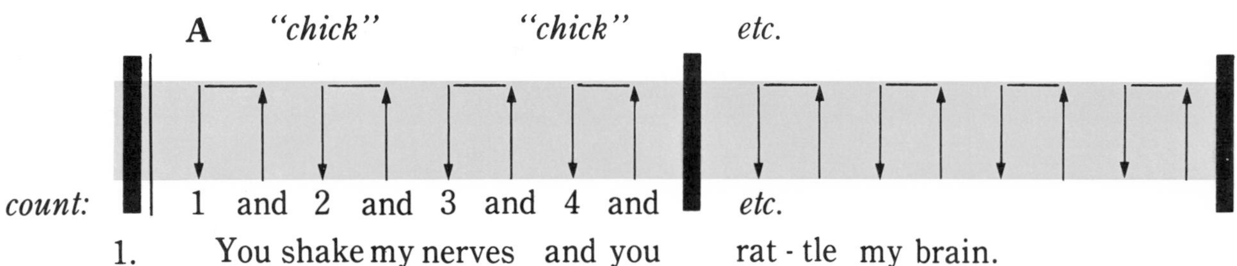
A "chick" "chick" etc.
count: 1 and 2 and 3 and 4 and etc.

1. You shake my nerves and you rat - tle my brain.
2. I laughed at love_ 'cause I thought it was fun-ny.

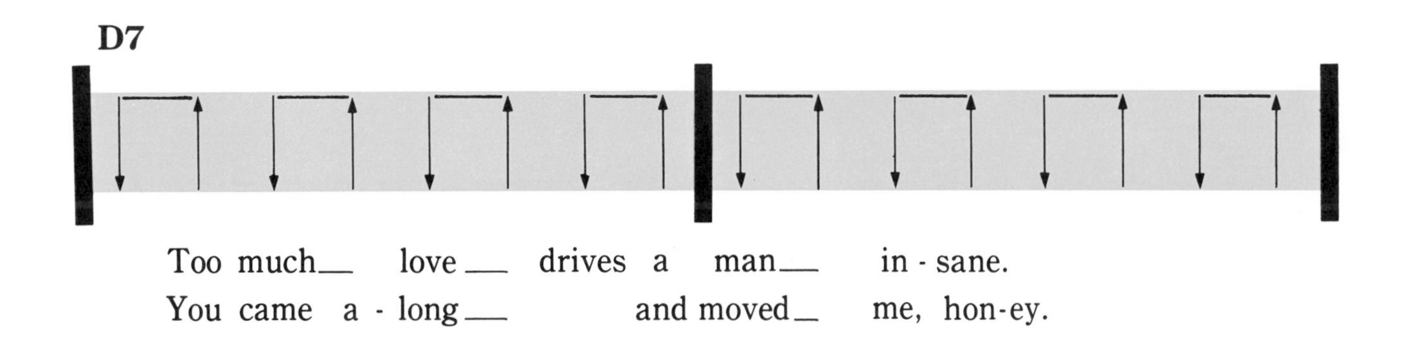
D7

Too much_ love_ drives a man_ in - sane.
You came a - long_ and moved_ me, hon-ey.

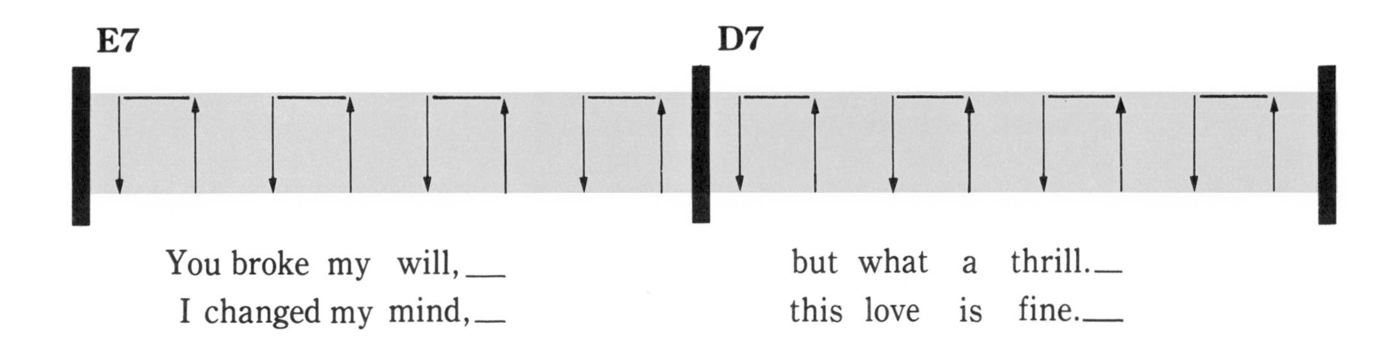
E7
D7

You broke my will,_ but what a thrill._
I changed my mind,_ this love is fine._

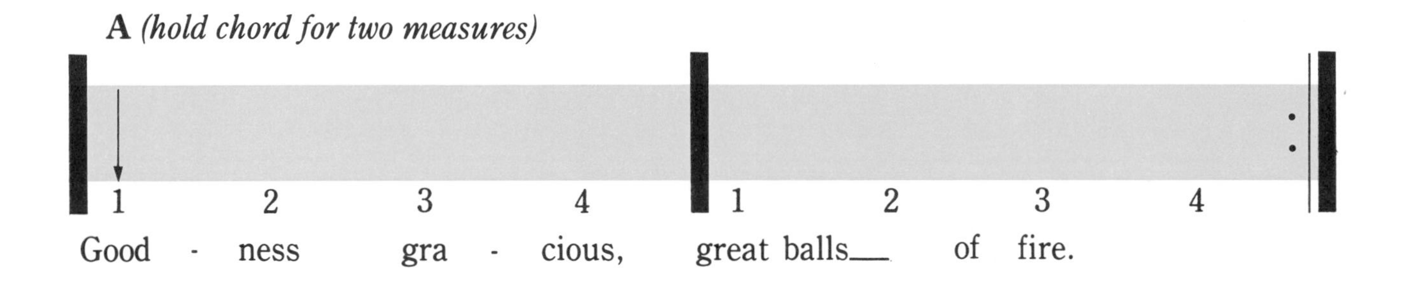
A (hold chord for two measures)
1 2 3 4 1 2 3 4

Good - ness gra - cious, great balls_ of fire.

Black Magic Woman

SANTANA

Carlos Santana brought a Latin influence into rock 'n' roll with great success. One of his most famous songs is "Black Magic Woman." We can play this song with our basic strum (down-up, down-up, down-up, down-up). First, let's learn one more new chord, **B7**.

B7

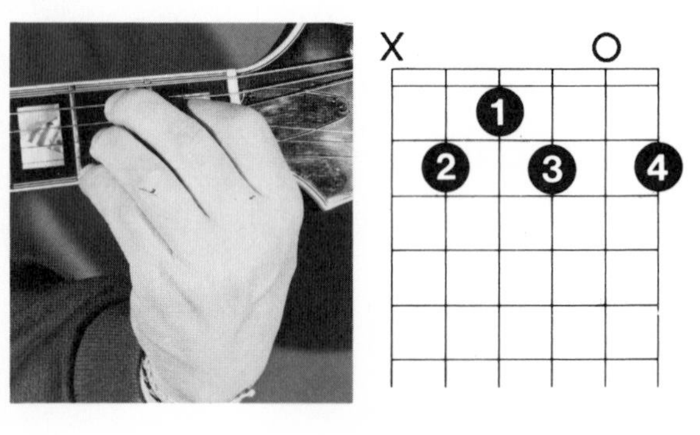
X
O
1
2
3
4

Black Magic Woman
By Peter Green

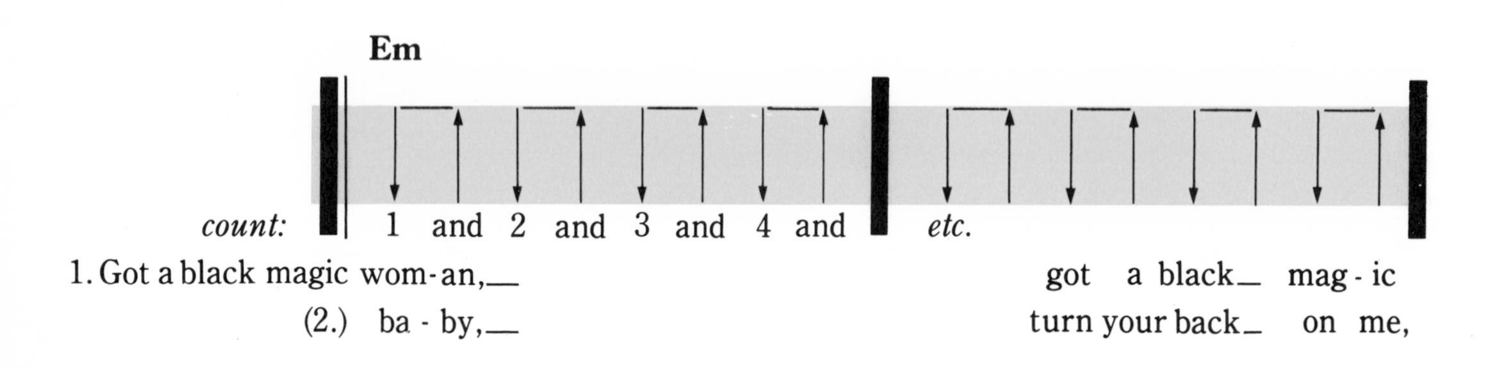
Em
count: 1 and 2 and 3 and 4 and *etc.*
1. Got a black magic wom-an,__ got a black_ mag - ic
(2.) ba - by,__ turn your back_ on me,

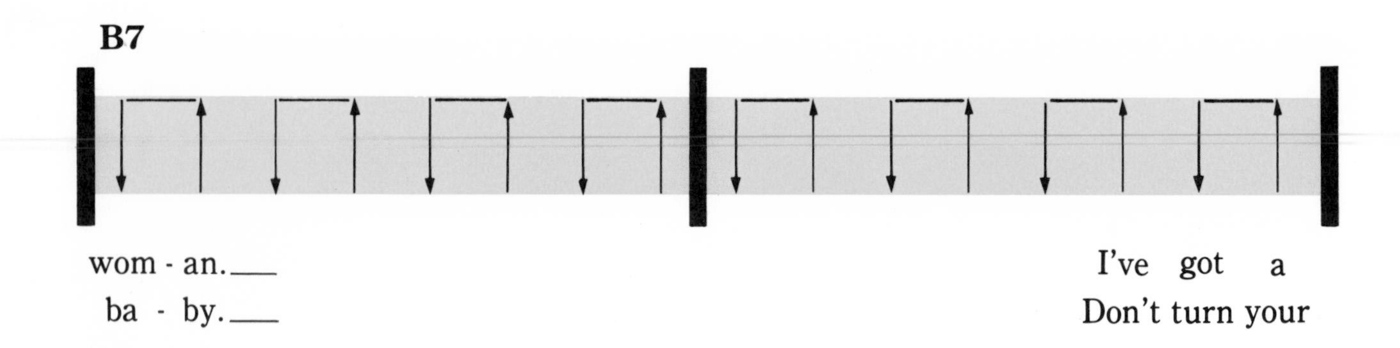
B7
wom - an.___ I've got a
ba - by.___ Don't turn your

Black Magic Woman *continued*

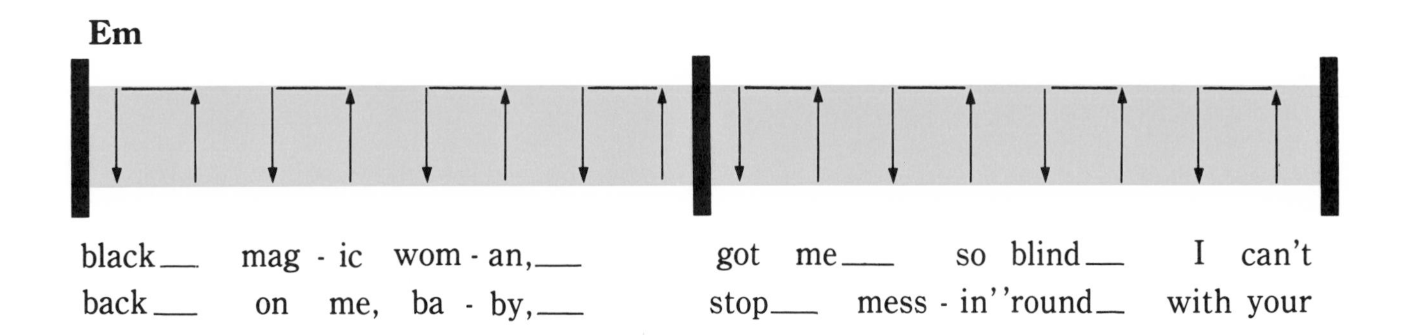
Em
black mag - ic wom - an, got me so blind I can't
back on me, ba - by, stop mess - in' 'round with your

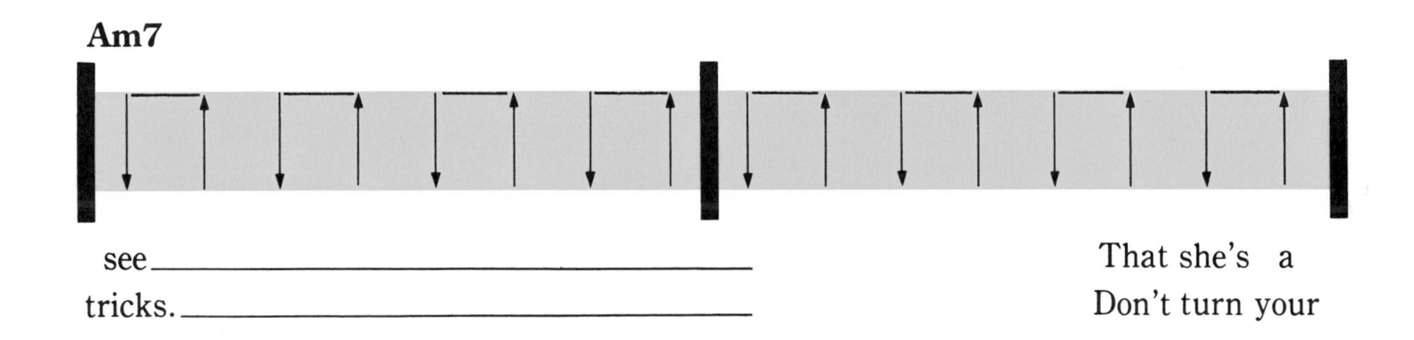
Am7
see That she's a
tricks. Don't turn your

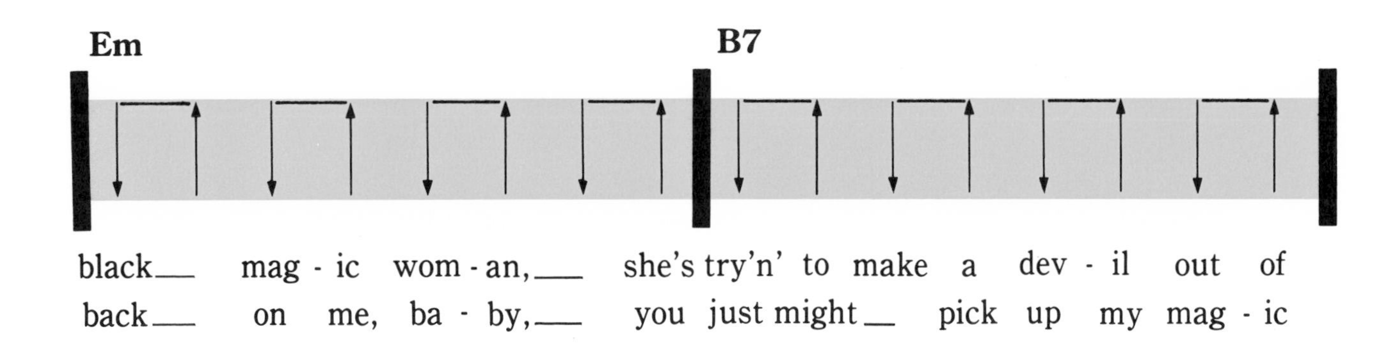
Em
B7
black mag - ic wom - an, she's try'n' to make a dev - il out of
back on me, ba - by, you just might pick up my mag - ic

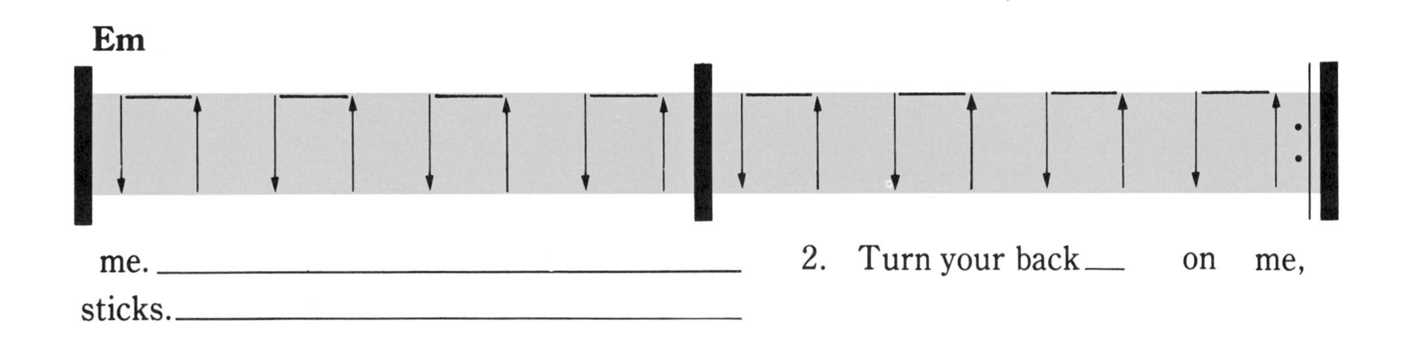
Em
me. 2. Turn your back on me,
sticks.

Johnny B. Goode

Chuck Berry is one of rock music's most influential guitarists and songwriters. His songs have become rock standards, and every rock guitarist should know them.

The one song that probably best captures the spirit of rock 'n' roll is "Johnny B. Goode." Because this song is so important, I want to show you two ways to play it. First, let's learn a new chord, **E.**

E

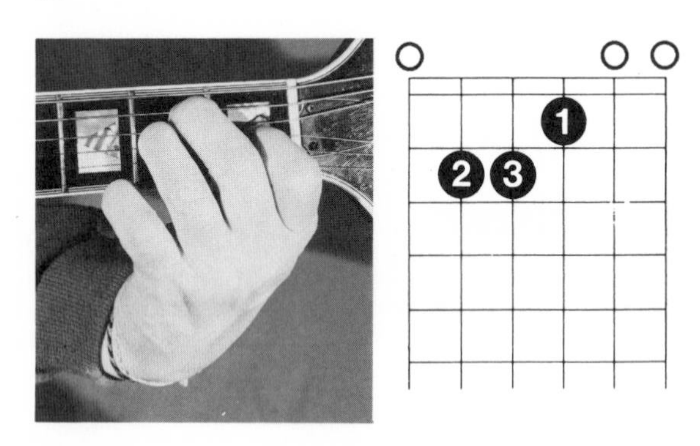

In this version of "Johnny B. Goode," use the down, down, down-up, down-up strumming pattern (Strumming Pattern 2).

Johnny B. Goode

Words and Music by Chuck Berry

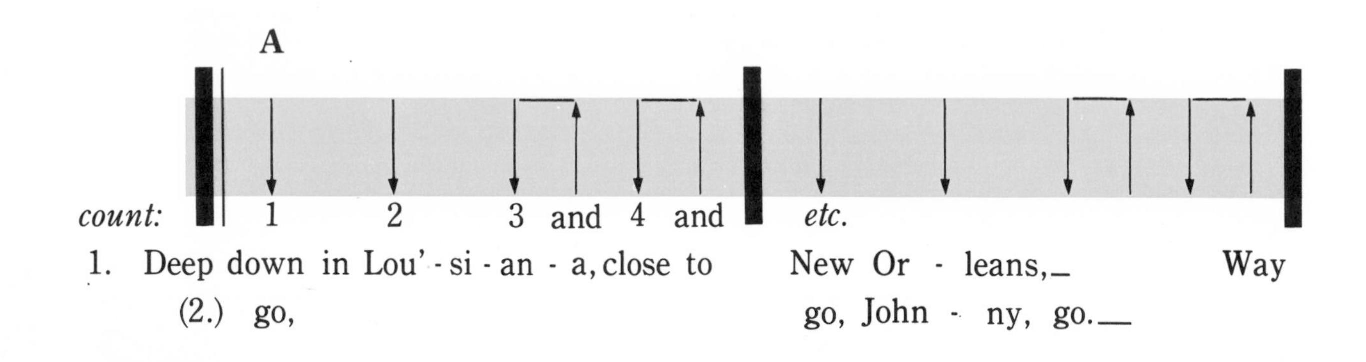
A
count: 1 2 3 and 4 and etc.
1. Deep down in Lou' - si - an - a, close to New Or - leans,_ Way
(2.) go, go, John - ny, go._

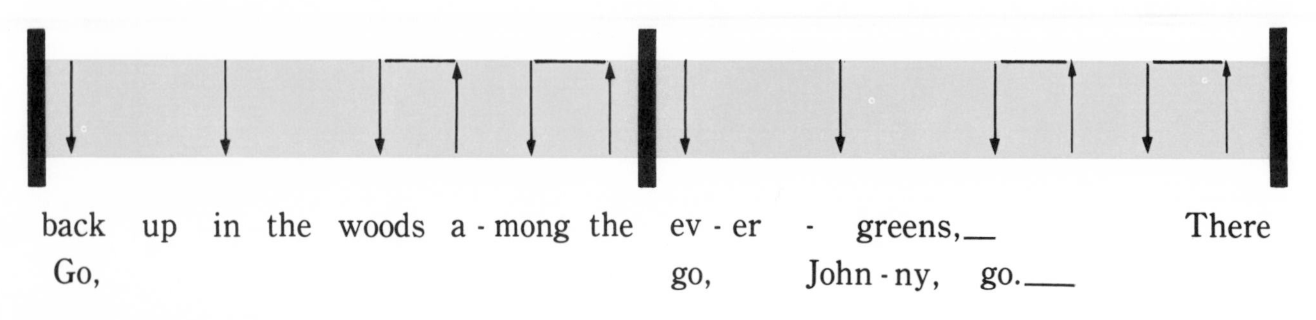
back up in the woods a - mong the ev - er - greens,_ There
Go, go, John - ny, go._

Johnny B. Goode *continued*

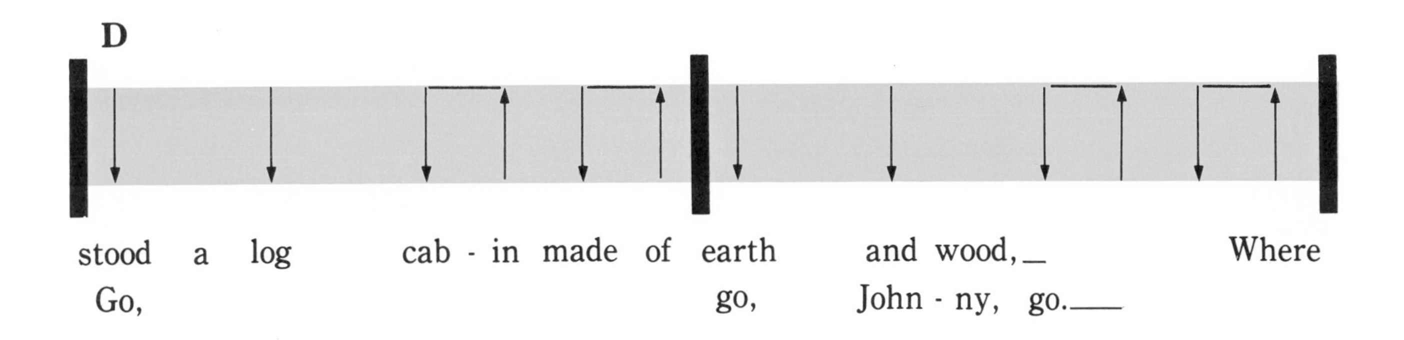
D
stood a log cab - in made of earth and wood,_ Where
Go, go, John - ny, go.___

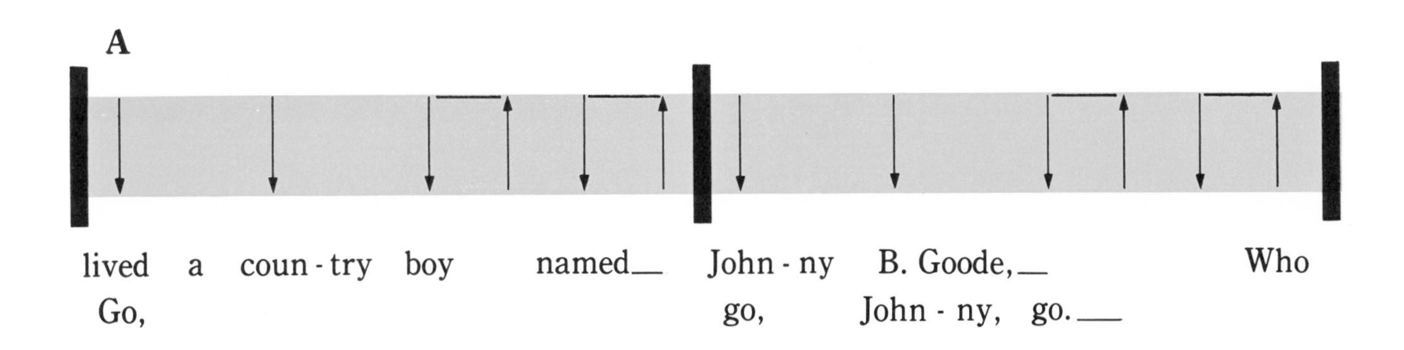
A
lived a coun - try boy named_ John - ny B. Goode,_ Who
Go, go, John - ny, go.___

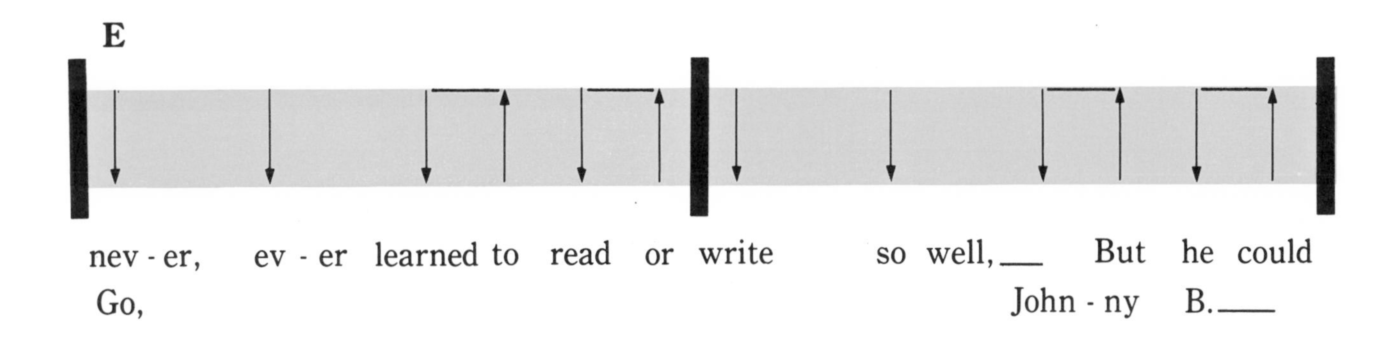
E
nev - er, ev - er learned to read or write so well,___ But he could
Go, John - ny B.___

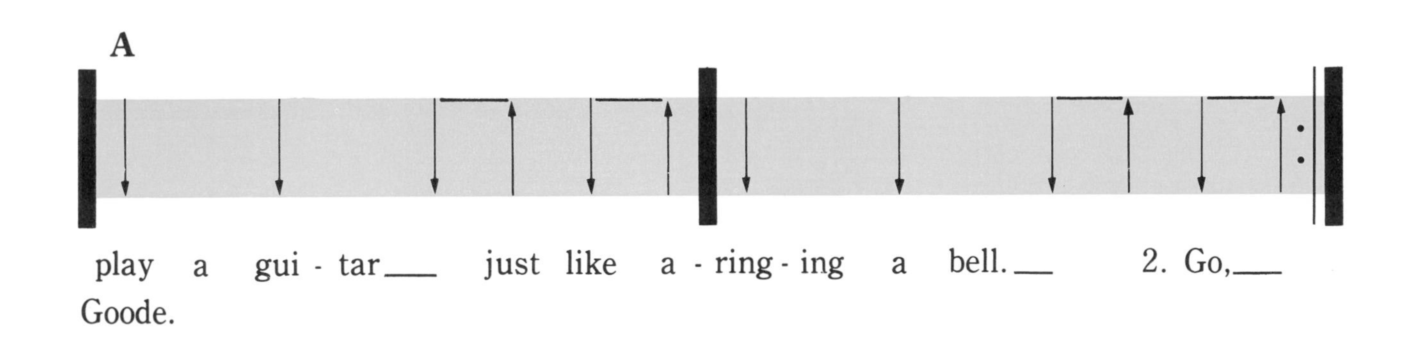
A
play a gui - tar___ just like a - ring - ing a bell.___ 2. Go,___
Goode.

In the next version of "Johnny B. Goode," instead of playing chords, we are going to play **riffs**.

A riff is a melodic fragment, usually very rhythmic, that can form the basic accompaniment for a song. The riff to use for "Johnny B. Goode" was made famous by Chuck Berry himself. In fact, it's often called the **Chuck Berry riff.**

You can play the riff instead of playing chords. Or, if a second guitarist is playing chords, you can play the riff as a lead guitar part.

"Johnny B. Goode" uses three chords: **A, D,** and **E.** The Chuck Berry riff can be substituted for each of these chords, as long as the riff is played on the proper strings. For example, to play the riff that goes with the **A** chord, place your first finger at the second fret of the fourth string. Now play two downstrokes, hitting only the fifth string (open) and the fourth string (fretted as indicated). Next add your third finger at the fourth fret of the fourth string (still holding down your first finger on the second fret) and play two more downstrokes. These four downstrokes are played in the same rhythm that you used for two down-up strums in the basic strum:

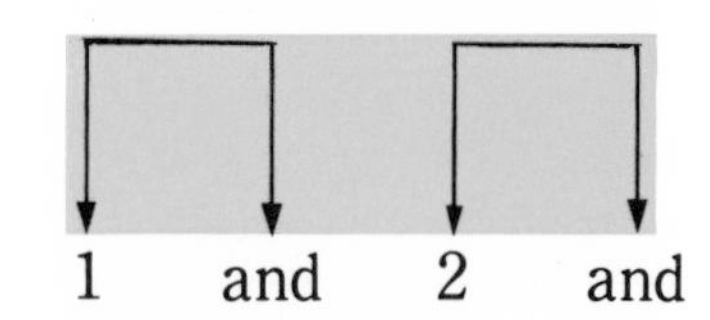
1
and
2
and

The diagram below shows the Chuck Berry riff (in **A**) as it is played on the neck.

Play these two strings only.

X O X X X

This finger stays down throughout.

This finger plays two off and two on.

Another way to show the same riff is to use a form of guitar notation called **tablature.** The six-line tablature staff graphically represents the six strings of the guitar, with the top line representing the high **E** string. Numbers designate the frets to be played, and a zero indicates an open string. As in standard notation, bar lines are used to group the beats into measures.

Here is how the Chuck Berry riff (in **A**) looks in tablature.

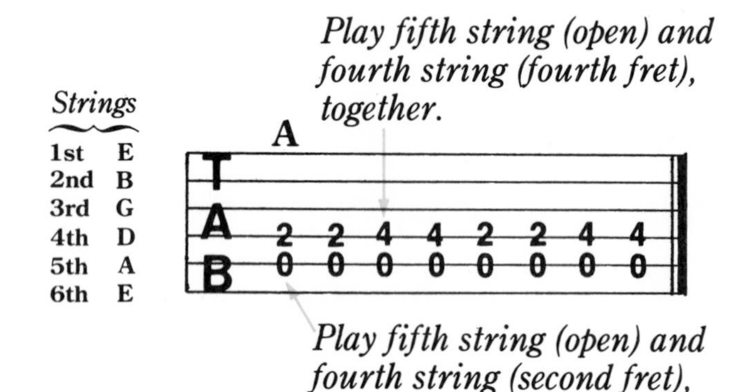
Play fifth string (open) and fourth string (fourth fret), together.
Strings
1st E
2nd B
3rd G
4th D
5th A
6th E
A
T
A
B
2 2 4 4 2 2 4 4
0 0 0 0 0 0 0 0
Play fifth string (open) and fourth string (second fret), together.

You can play the Chuck Berry riff that goes with the **D** chord by playing the same finger pattern that went with the **A** chord, except on strings four and three.

In diagram form the riff in **D** looks like this:

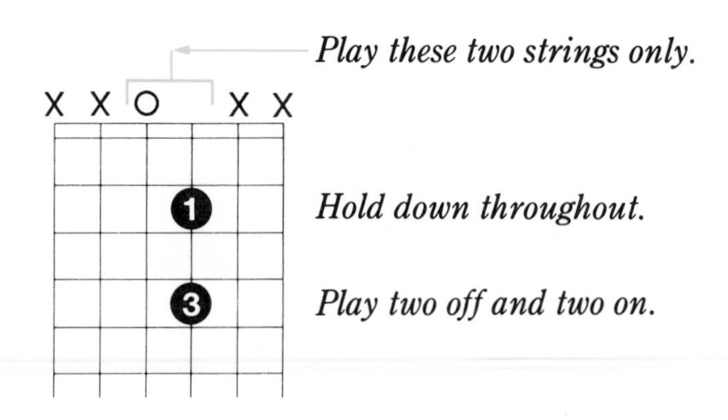
Play these two strings only.
X X O X X
Hold down throughout.
Play two off and two on.

In tablature it looks like this:

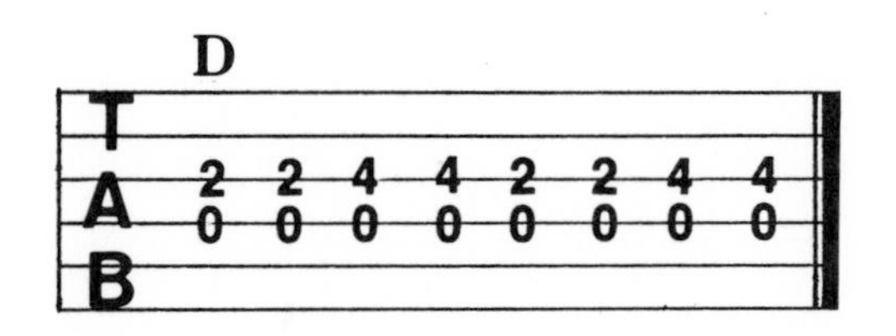
D
T
A
B
2 2 4 4 2 2 4 4
0 0 0 0 0 0 0 0

Again, the same finger pattern is used to play the Chuck Berry riff on an **E** chord, except now you'll use strings six and five.

Here is how the **E** riff looks in diagram form and in tablature:

O X X X X

Play these two strings only.

Hold down throughout.

Play two off and two on.

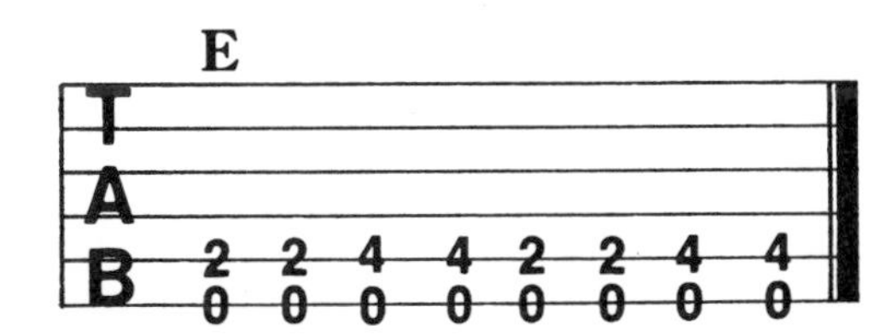
E
T
A
B
2 2 4 4 2 2 4 4
0 0 0 0 0 0 0 0

Now we're ready to play "Johnny B. Goode" using riffs instead of chords. When you get it down, I'm sure you'll hear how these riffs can really make the difference between just strumming along and really rocking. Remember to play downstrokes throughout, and play as rhythmically as possible. Also, try to associate each riff with its proper chord symbol (placed above the tablature staff) so that as you progress you'll be able to substitute these riffs for the normal chords.

Riffs

Johnny B. Goode

A
1. Deep down in Lou'-si - an - a, close to New Or - leans, Way
(2.) go, go, John-ny, go.
back up in the woods a-mong the ev - er - greens, There
Go, go, John-ny, go.
D
stood a log cab - in made of earth and wood, Where
Go, go, John-ny, go.
A
lived a coun-try boy named John - ny B. Goode, Who
Go, go, John-ny, go.
E
nev - er, ev - er learned to read or write so well, But he could
Go, John-ny B.
A
play a gui - tar just like a - ring-ing a bell. 2. Go,
Goode.

Sus4 to the Floor

Sometimes it's possible to play a chord and a riff at the same time. One way to do this is to alternately add and remove a finger on one string while strumming a chord. For example, with a **D** chord, you can add your fourth finger to the third fret of the first string. This changes the chord from **D** to **D Suspended Fourth (Dsus4).**

D

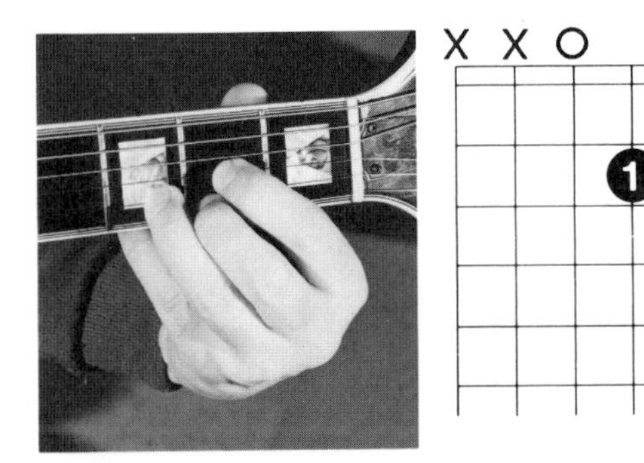
X X O

Dsus4

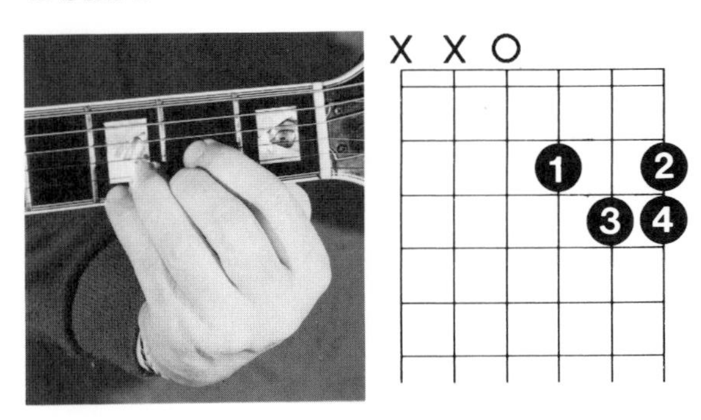
X X O

With a **C** chord, you can add your fourth finger to the third fret of the fourth string, producing a **Csus4** chord. (When strumming **Csus4,** tilt your first finger so that it gently presses against the first string, blocking out the sound.)

C

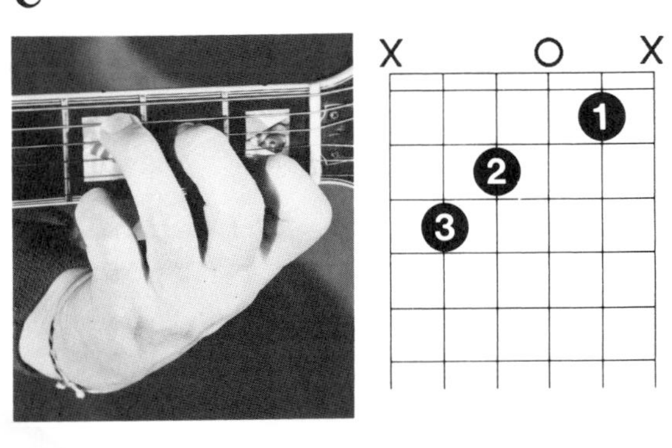
X O X

Csus4

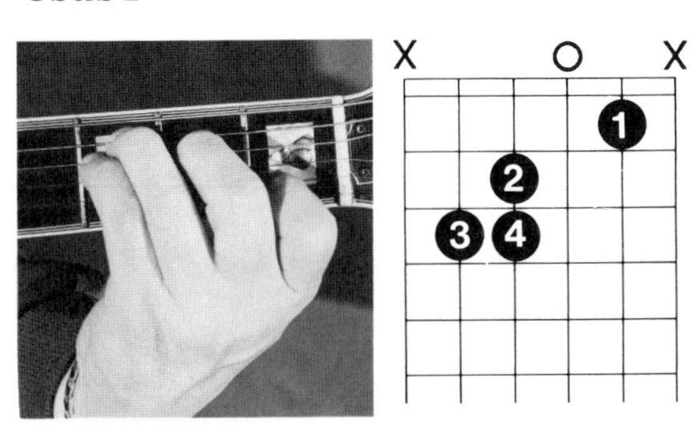
X O X

"Sus4 to the Floor" is a piece I've written to get you used to playing **sus4** chords. You'll also play two new strumming patterns. The first pattern (in the first eight measures) is a down, down-up, down, down strum. The second pattern (in the last eight measures) is a "start-stop" rhythm that can be very exciting, especially when playing with a drummer.

To play this start-stop pattern, play a downstroke on beat one, then rest (don't play) on beats two and three, then play a downstroke on beat four. The important thing to remember is that while resting, don't let the sound (from beat one) carry over into the empty beats. This can be accomplished by covering the strings with your right hand until it's time to strum again. This way, your left-hand fingers can remain in place. When done correctly, this effect produces a very rhythmic feel.

Riffs

Sus4 to the Floor

Music by Steve Tarshis

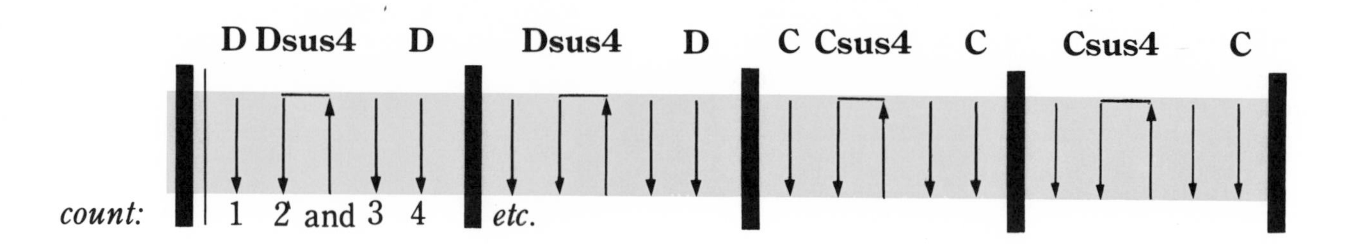
D Dsus4 D
Dsus4 D
C Csus4 C
Csus4 C
count:
1 2 and 3 4
etc.

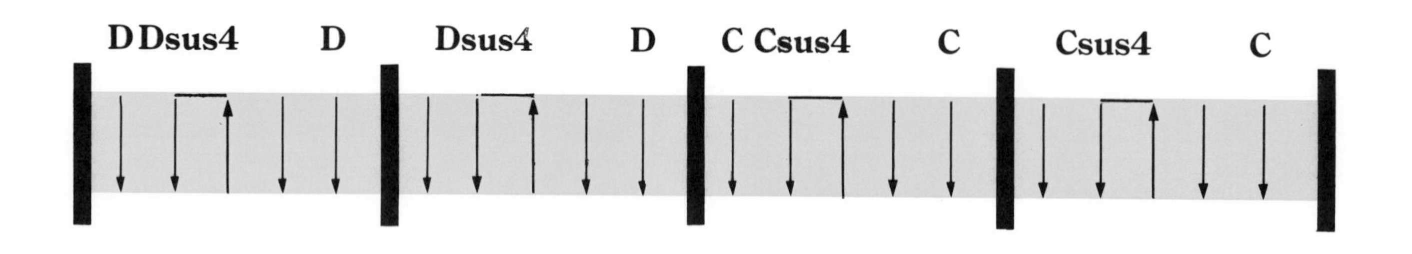
D Dsus4 D
Dsus4 D
C Csus4 C
Csus4 C

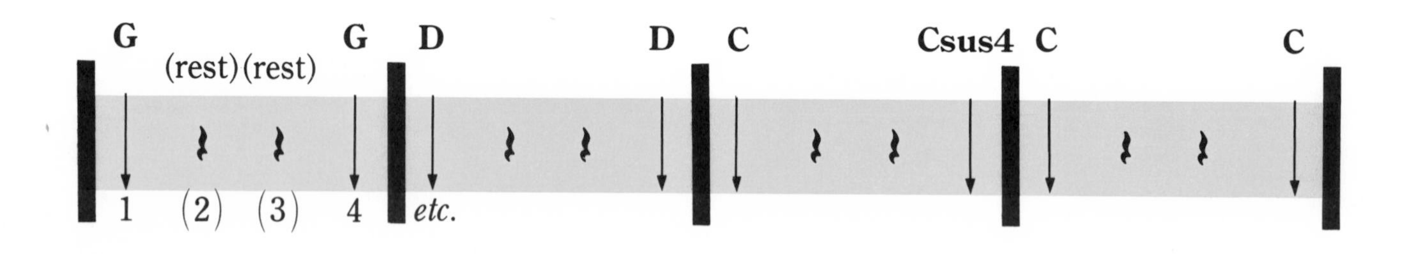
G
(rest) (rest)
G
D
D
C
Csus4 C
C
1 (2) (3) 4
etc.

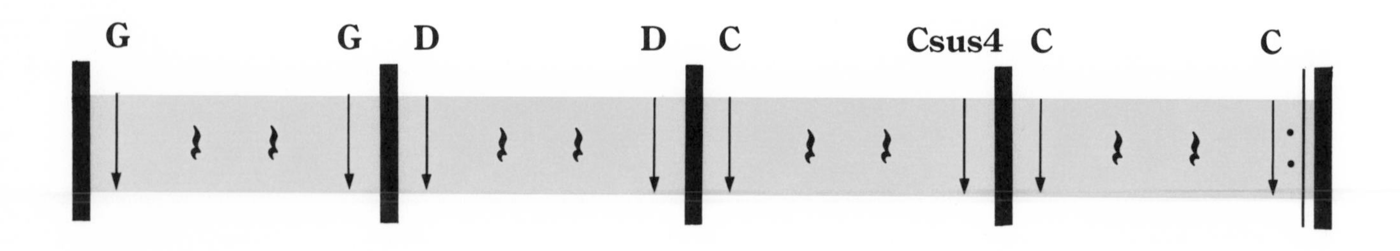
G
G
D
D
C
Csus4 C
C

Closing Comments

That's it for now. **Book 1** has given you what I hope will be a good foundation for rock 'n' roll guitar playing. The best, however, is yet to come. Practice what you've learned in **Book 1,** and I'll see you in **Book 2.** Remember, the more you practice, the more you'll rock!